A FRANK BETZ ASSOCIATES INC. COLLECTION

# MAIN-FLOOR MASTER SUITES

# 65 BEST-SELLING HOME PLANS
## WITH MASTER BEDROOMS ON THE MAIN FLOOR

Bright yellow and red toile fabrics create a cheerful master bedroom suite. Large windows allow sunlight to pour in.

See more of the Westhampton on page 124.

# FRANK BETZ
# INTRODUCTION

You were the inspiration for this anthology — you, and those like you, that welcome simplicity and sophistication, ease and elegance, practicality and pampering — those who realize you don't have to sacrifice beauty for function or form for grace. Sometime during your search for a home, you thought about what was important to you: a home tailored to your lifestyle, a home that reflects you, a home designed to make your day-to-day living easier. So, inspired by your needs and wishes, we present *Main-Floor Master Suites* — a collection of home plans for every family make-up and every stage of life.

Divided into two sections, One-Story Living and Main-Level Living, *Main-Floor Master Suites* presents an unmatched collection of home plans created through careful research and design to meet your needs today and help you prepare for the distant tomorrow. With open, versatile floor plans surrounded by stylish, low-maintenance exteriors, *Main-Floor Master Suites* showcases one of the most requested features in a new home — a main-level master suite designed to provide you with the convenience, comfort and privacy you seek.

Tonight, as you drift off to sleep, we wish you sweet dreams as you contemplate your new dream home! ▪

Built-in shelving and a well-positioned shelf above the sofa are perfect for displaying family treasures and heirlooms.

See more of the Northbrook on page 48.

# TABLE OF CONTENTS

A DESIGNS DIRECT PUBLISHING BOOK

presented by

**FRANK**
**BETZ**
**ASSOCIATES**
**I N C.**

Betz Publishing, LLC.
2401 Lake Park Drive, Suite 250
Smyrna, GA 30080
888-717-3003  |  www.mainfloormastersuites.com

Floor plans and elevations are subject to change. Floor plan dimensions are approximate. Consult working drawings for actual dimensions and information. Elevations are artists' conceptions.

Frank Betz – *Chairman*

Russell Moody – *President*

Laura Segers – *Editor-in-Chief*

Allen Bennetts – *Illustrator*

Joshua Thomas – *Art Director*

Paula Powers, Sarah Hockman – *Writers*

Bryan Willy/Bryan Willy Photography, Happy Terrebone/Terrebone Photography – *Photographers*


Prepress services by DMG Inc., Atlanta
Printed by Toppan Printing Company, Hong Kong


ISBN   1 – 9 3 2 5 5 3 – 1 2 – 6

First Printing, September 2005

Copyright © 2005 Betz Publishing, LLC

An equestrian theme was chosen for the décor of this vaulted bonus room — the perfect place for family movie time or reading a good book.

See more of the Westhampton on page 124.

# REST ASSURED

Life keeps you busy, and most of us enjoy a very active lifestyle. Acting as chauffer to and from your kids' after-school activities, taking that action-filled vacation, not being able to stay out of the office even though you've retired — are among the things that give us a sense of purpose and fulfillment. But at the end of the day, fulfillment doesn't mean we're living the easy life.

As you search for a new home, you can find a plan designed to help you live easier. Understanding and designing for the way families live is an evolutionary process, involving much research, observation and simply asking people what they need. Take the addition of the second bathroom that came after years of waiting in line at the only bathroom door. Think of how this room has changed from being another family bathroom — that the parents still had to wait to use — into the larger bathroom that is part of a beautiful master suite. Parents knew if they were running late in the mornings, the kids were also going to be late. Finally, second-floor masters moved to the main floor of the home, and now, a main-floor master suite is one of the features most requested by homeowners.

"Metrics" is the current buzz word in business — measuring and rating performance levels across the board. Have you ever wondered what would happen if you applied the same philosophy to your home's performance level, starting with the room where most of your living occurs, whether asleep or awake? Providing convenience, comfort and privacy, a main-floor master suite creates a haven of refuge from the hustle and bustle of everyday life, and a space that can truly make a difference in your life.

Faux-finished wainscoting provides stark contrast with the dark red walls in this formal dining room. Wrought-iron sconces highlight the rich tones of the walls.

See more of the Hennefield on page 58.

Choosing different finishes on cabinetry is popular with decorators today. The olive-painted island stands alone as compared to the stained finish on the rest of the kitchen cabinetry.

**See more of the Briarcliff Cottage on page 66.**

# CONVENIENCE

When was the last time you had to run down the stairs, interrupting your morning routine, in order to retrieve a clothing item you needed to wear from the laundry room? If it's been a while, you've probably realized the convenience of having the master suite located where all of your day-to-day living occurs. If not, you've probably come to realize what a difference a main-floor master suite could make to your quality of life.

How many times have you stopped your morning routine to go downstairs and prepare breakfast only to return to your bedroom later feeling a bit more rushed? When was the last time you left your wallet on the nightstand and remembered it as you were darting out the front door? A marathon runner knows the difference a few seconds can make, and reducing the number of steps it takes to go from the master suite to the kitchen, or elsewhere, is important. Seconds add up, which is why step-saving design elements such as main-floor master suites add such convenience to modern-day living.

Think about the tasks that occur in a master suite: cleaning the master bedroom and bath, packing or unpacking a suitcase, putting away toiletries after a visit to the market, and so on. How much easier would it be to not face the stairs every time you had your hands full? It is the little things that add to your quality of life, and why main-floor master suites are essential elements of convenience.

Ionic columns on paneled bases as well as ceiling delineation provide the right separation between sleeping and sitting areas in this master suite.

See more of the Castlegate on page 150.

Many life-coaches stress the need to remove unnecessary clutter and obstacles, and take a simpler view of life in order to elevate your quality of living. What if you applied the same principle to your home's design? It would result in life-enhancing features such as a main-floor master suite.

Let's face it, as we age, we don't have the energy of our youth. We may move a little slower. Our joints may become a little stiffer, and there comes a time when we must be as prepared as possible for whatever the future holds.

When you have an ache or are fatigued, the last thing you want to do is walk up and down a flight of stairs several times a day. You want to exert your energy where it counts: playing a round on the golf course, taking the kids to the park or presenting that huge proposal to the board. After a long day of work and play, you want your rest to come easy.

Main-floor master suites provide a realm of personalized comfort that is unmatched by any other room in the house. There's peace in knowing you're a few steps away from the great room, kitchen or home office, so when you're ready for bed, it's easily accessible.

When you remove unnecessary obstacles, safety increases. Many home injuries involve the stairs. It's as simple as missing one step, and before you know it, you're at the bottom with only minor injuries if you're lucky. Home accidents almost always occur when performing the most routine tasks like walking up the stairs after a trip to the drycleaners and having a hanger catch on the railing. The next thing you know, you've tripped and caught yourself, but you'll spend the next few minutes gathering your pressed clothes from off of the stairs and the next few days nursing a sore wrist.

Comfort means more than a feeling of well-being. It also means the capacity to give physical ease. As you consider your new home, think about what comfort means and how a main-floor master suite fits into the picture.

A spacious bay window adds just the right
amount of room needed for his and her chairs.
This provides the occupants a private space
within the confines of their own bedroom.

See more of the Northbrook on page 48.

# PRIVACY

Master suites have taken on additional responsibilities other than providing room for sleep. How many times have you heard or spoken the phrase "the walls have ears," and where do you normally go when you want to have a private conversation or be alone with your spouse? This is why master bedrooms have always been reserved for private conversations and intimacy. Yet second-floor masters do not always afford a real sense of privacy, and this need for privacy was among the first reasons why couples wanted to move the master suite from the second floor.

Privacy is multi-faceted. It also involves keeping noise out for peaceful sleep. As children become teenagers, it seems as if their capacity to make noise increases. Volume levels rise on radios and televisions. Phone conversations last into the nighttime, and these things can affect a good night's sleep for many parents.

What if you don't have children or are an empty-nester? Maybe you like to have guests come and visit, or maybe you have converted an upstairs' secondary bedroom into a home office. Placing the master suite on the first floor affords you and your guests privacy, and you're not kept awake by your spouse's late-night working.

In homes that have two or more floors, additional floors are often smaller in square footage than main-floors, so when all of the bedrooms are upstairs, there is less room to incorporate design elements such as closets that act as noise buffers. For one-level homes, master suites that are located near secondary bedrooms and other rooms can be positioned for privacy, and design elements are much more easily planned. As you're choosing a home plan, bear in mind your privacy requirements and how the home meets those needs.

Arches with moldings and wood columns create the entrance into this living room area. Stained casework contrasts with the vivid white wood mantel and moldings.

See more of the Woodcliffe on page 138.

NOW THAT YOU'VE CONSIDERED CONVENIENCE, COMFORT AND PRIVACY, THINK ABOUT THE WAY YOU LIVE AND HOW THE MASTER SUITE'S SCALE AND LOCATION WILL BEST FIT YOUR LIFESTYLE.

## SCALE

It's true that lots are becoming smaller, and some people are adding a basement and/or second-floor to get the square footage they require. But how do you know how much space you need, especially in the master suite? It really depends on what you're going to do with the space.

As more and more people are discovering how they want their master bedroom to live, master suites are becoming private sanctuaries. In some cases people are removing desks, media equipment and exercise machines in order to create more tranquil environments. With the removal of these items, people have realized that they didn't need as much space as they thought they did.

On the other hand, some people want these items in their master suites, because they are convenient for the way they live. A writer may wish to have a desk close by the bed when he or she is struck with late-night inspiration. An avid exerciser might want to wake up and work out first thing in the morning. Some one else might find it easier to fall asleep with the television creating low background noise.

So think about how you use your master suite. Do you need a lot of space for pieces other than your bed and dresser? Are there other areas in your home where you would consider moving a treadmill or desk? Do you like to watch movies in bed? Asking yourself questions like this will help you choose a master suite that is scaled for the way you live and in proportion to the rest of the home.

## LOCATION

Think about your daily routines. Are you an early riser that likes to be close to the kitchen in order to have some quiet time with a cup of morning coffee? If so, you might like to have a master bedroom that's off of the kitchen or breakfast nook. Or maybe you like to sleep with the bedroom door open and would prefer a more secluded location away from the gathering rooms.

Going a step further, think about how your home will be placed on its lot. Do you like to sleep in? If so, you may want to take note of the solar patterns in your area and position your house to avoid the bright morning sun. Also, see how your home will be positioned in relation to neighboring houses. You may be able to have your house plan modified in order to move your master bedroom windows if needed.

A main-floor master suite already places you in a better location for convenience, comfort and privacy, so think about how you want it to relate to other areas of your home. For example, if you're planning on having children, and would like the nursery located on the same floor as the master bedroom, consider a home plan with a flexible study/bedroom, which would allow your infant to be near you. As your child grows, you can move him or her into an upstairs "big boy or girl" bedroom and convert the bedroom/study to an office. If an older loved one comes to live with you, you may desire a study/bedroom near the master suite in order to provide any needed assistance.

A large-screen television and an art niche are the focal point in this living room. Rich tones of red and gold create a sense of warmth in the room.

See more of the Northbrook on page 48.

Now that you've considered scale and location, think about the obvious "icing on the cake" that comes within the main-floor master suite — the convenient, comfortable, private master bath — the retreat within a retreat. Here you can have your garden tub, separate shower, dual vanities and so on, and although it will only be a short distance away from where your day-to-day living occurs, it will feel like a different world that's easy to reach. With plenty of room for two, it's the perfect place to start and end your day.

While looking through the pages of this book, choose a style that best reflects your personality and still maintains the integrity of your environment — whether you're in the heart of the country or the heart of the city. In this book, you won't have to worry about choosing a plan only to find it has a second-floor master suite. We designed and selected these home plans because they all have main-level masters and every one offers a way to live easier.

Just remember as you flip through these pages, ask yourself questions about the way you live and be sure to ask your spouse and other family members how they want to live. Together, you can choose a home plan that is designed to enhance your whole family's lifestyle. Sleep well! ▪

Chic blends of gilded tones, deep-pile fabrics and tapestries create a look of modern comfort in the master bedroom.

See more of the Briarcliff Cottage on page 66.

## ONE-STORY LIVING

One-Story Living features a selection of home plans that are ageless yet modern. Inspired by a desire to keep living simple, while creating a sense of place, these homes are designed to be livable, versatile and indulging, as witnessed by the attentive master suites. Featuring signature characteristics of Frank Betz Associates' renowned style, this section highlights a variety of square footages and home styles.

From stone and cedar cottages that hint of far-away places to brick traditionals that create a stately moment in time, architecturally-detailed exteriors welcome family and friends alike. With an emphasis on enhancing lifestyles and complementing the way families live, these floor plans provide open, innovative spaces with charming interior features, and each home offers plans that open easily to the outdoors.

One-Story Living is dedicated to those who want their home to live easy — no matter their make-up, age or interest. ▪

# River Hill

Plan Number: MLFB04-3915
Price Code: B

The façade of the River Hill is like a friendly invitation to come in and see more. Cheery dormers atop a covered porch extend a warm welcome to visitors. A vaulted family room is the focal point from the foyer, with a cozy fireplace as its backdrop. The master suite is secluded from the other bedrooms giving homeowners privacy. A serving bar in the kitchen caters to the breakfast area and family room – convenient for entertaining. Finishing the optional second floor adds a bedroom and bath, as well as a bonus room that can be used at the homeowner's discretion. ■

Foundations Available: Basement, Crawl or Slab

*Rear elevation*

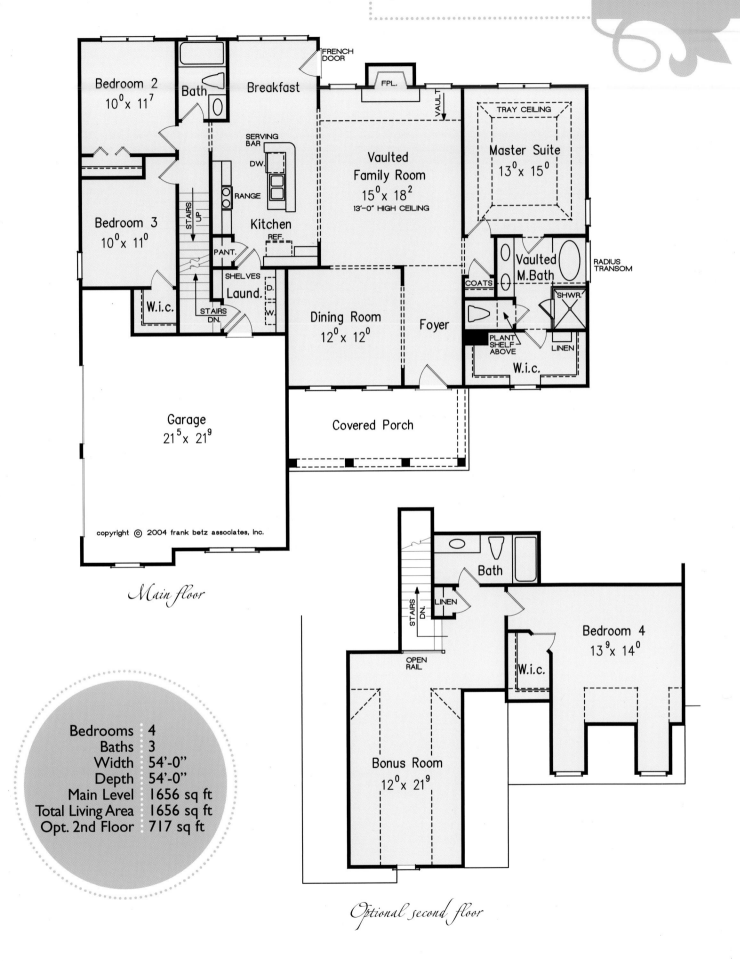

Bedroom 2
$10^0$ x $11^7$

Bath

Breakfast

FRENCH DOOR

FPL.

VAULT

TRAY CEILING

Master Suite
$13^0$ x $15^0$

SERVING BAR

DW.

RANGE

Kitchen

Vaulted
Family Room
$15^0$ x $18^2$
$13'$-$0''$ HIGH CEILING

Bedroom 3
$10^0$ x $11^0$

STAIRS UP

PANT.

REF.

SHELVES

W.i.c.

STAIRS DN.

Laund.

D.

W.

Dining Room
$12^0$ x $12^0$

Foyer

Vaulted M.Bath

RADIUS TRANSOM

COATS

SHWR.

PLANT SHELF ABOVE

LINEN

W.i.c.

Garage
$21^5$ x $21^9$

Covered Porch

copyright © 2004 frank betz associates, inc.

*Main floor*

STAIRS DN.

Bath

LINEN

OPEN RAIL

Bedroom 4
$13^9$ x $14^0$

W.i.c.

Bonus Room
$12^0$ x $21^9$

*Optional second floor*

Bedrooms : 4
Baths : 3
Width : 54'-0"
Depth : 54'-0"
Main Level : 1656 sq ft
Total Living Area : 1656 sq ft
Opt. 2nd Floor : 717 sq ft

# Stoneheath

Plan Number: MLFB04-3814
Price Code: B

The Stoneheath's clever combination of stone with board-and-batten siding creates that friendly curb appeal that many of today's homeowners are in search of. Guests will appreciate the covered entry on rainy days. Ideal for entertaining, the breakfast, living and dining rooms inconspicuously connect to create easy traffic flow from one room to the next. Just off the garage, a handy sink is designed into the laundry room, making the perfect stopping point to clean up before proceeding inside. An optional bonus room is available that easily finishes into a fourth bedroom or children's recreation room. ■

Foundations Available: Basement or Crawl

*Rear elevation*

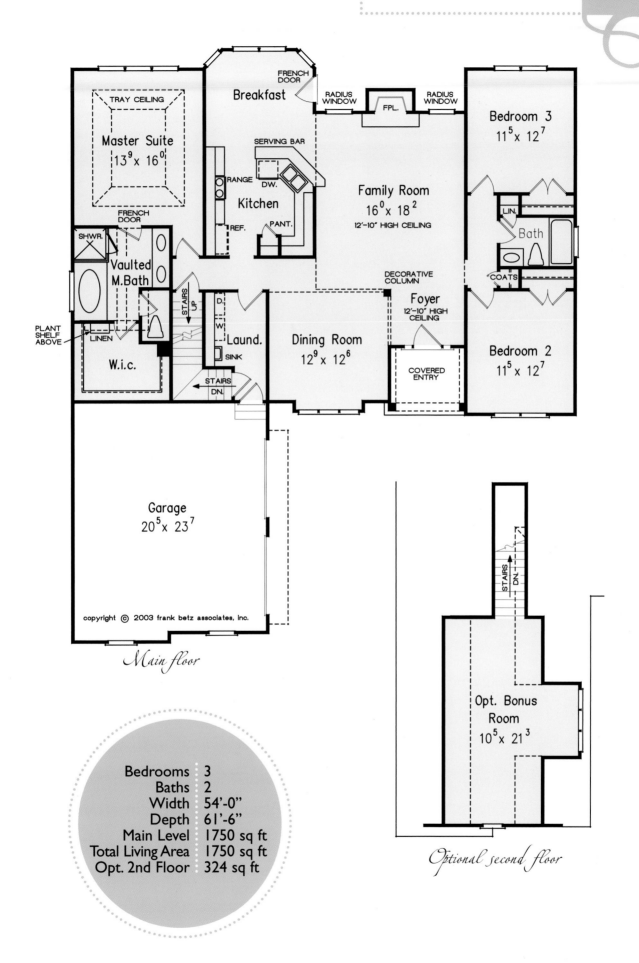

TRAY CEILING

**Master Suite**
$13^9$ x $16^0$

FRENCH DOOR

**Breakfast**

FRENCH DOOR

RADIUS WINDOW    FPL.    RADIUS WINDOW

**Bedroom 3**
$11^5$ x $12^7$

SERVING BAR

RANGE    DW.

**Kitchen**

REF.    PANT.

**Family Room**
$16^0$ x $18^2$
12'-10" HIGH CEILING

LIN.

**Bath**

SHWR.

**Vaulted M. Bath**

FRENCH DOOR

STAIRS UP

COATS

PLANT SHELF ABOVE

LINEN

D. W.

**Laund.**

SINK

DECORATIVE COLUMN

**Foyer**
12'-10" HIGH CEILING

**Bedroom 2**
$11^5$ x $12^7$

**W.i.c.**

STAIRS DN.

**Dining Room**
$12^9$ x $12^6$

COVERED ENTRY

**Garage**
$20^5$ x $23^7$

copyright © 2003 frank betz associates, inc.

*Main floor*

STAIRS DN.

**Opt. Bonus Room**
$10^5$ x $21^3$

*Optional second floor*

| | |
|---|---|
| Bedrooms | 3 |
| Baths | 2 |
| Width | 54'-0" |
| Depth | 61'-6" |
| Main Level | 1750 sq ft |
| Total Living Area | 1750 sq ft |
| Opt. 2nd Floor | 324 sq ft |

# Brookhollow

Plan Number: MLFB04-3694
Price Code: C

Unique artistic details are used on the façade of the Brookhollow giving it an alluring cottage feel. Copper window accents, brick and an arched covered entry come together to create a warm welcome for family and guests. The main living area is airy and unobtrusive, with decorative columns serving as the subtle border of the dining room. Radius windows on each side of the fireplace allow the natural light to pour into this living space. The master suite is oversized, with a private sitting area emphasized by an arched opening. ▪

Foundations Available: Basement, Crawl or Slab

*Rear elevation*

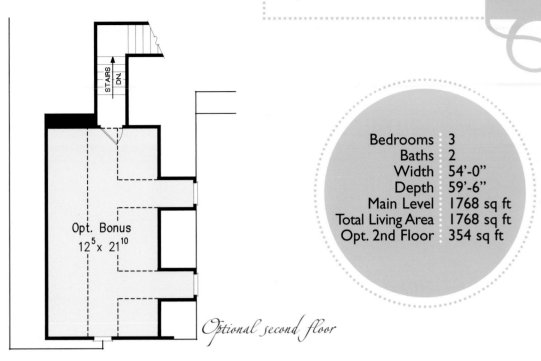

*Optional second floor*

Opt. Bonus
12⁵ x 21¹⁰

| | |
|---|---|
| Bedrooms | 3 |
| Baths | 2 |
| Width | 54'-0" |
| Depth | 59'-6" |
| Main Level | 1768 sq ft |
| Total Living Area | 1768 sq ft |
| Opt. 2nd Floor | 354 sq ft |

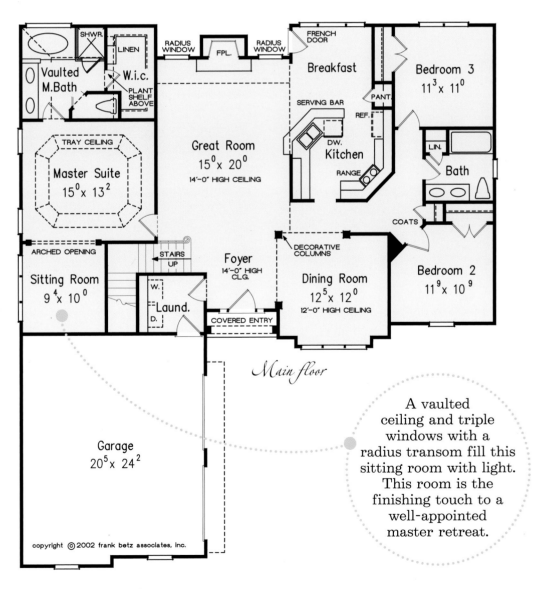

*Main floor*

A vaulted ceiling and triple windows with a radius transom fill this sitting room with light. This room is the finishing touch to a well-appointed master retreat.

copyright © 2002 frank betz associates, inc.

# Kenmore Park

Plan Number: MLFB04-3700
Price Code: C

A traditional combination of brick and siding is a backdrop for the rocking-chair front porch that beautifies the front of the Kenmore Park. Oval and radius windows provide that fresh, homey appeal sought after today. Inside, a clean and simple split-bedroom design features three bedrooms and two baths. A versatile serving bar accommodates the breakfast area and family room, providing additional seating or serving space for gatherings with family or friends. Optional space opens the opportunity for a fourth bedroom and third bath, ideal for a home office or guest accommodations. A storage niche in the garage is perfectly sized for gardening tools. ■

Foundations Available: Basement, Crawl or Slab

*Rear elevation*

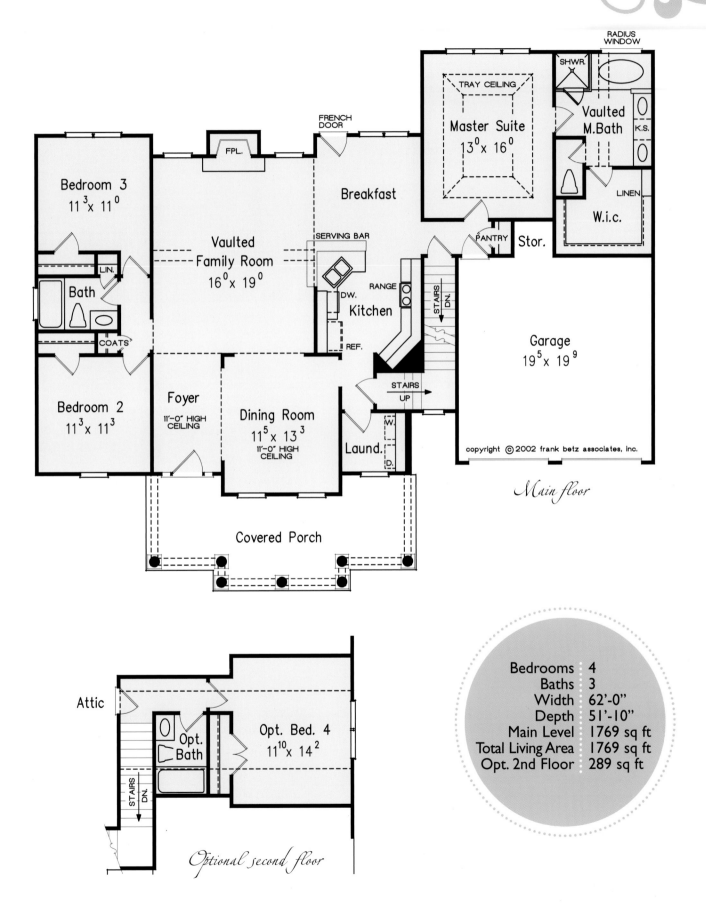

Bedroom 3
11³ x 11⁰

FPL.

FRENCH DOOR

Master Suite
13⁰ x 16⁰

TRAY CEILING

SHWR.

RADIUS WINDOW

Vaulted M.Bath

K.S.

LINEN

W.i.c.

Breakfast

Vaulted Family Room
16⁰ x 19⁰

SERVING BAR

DW.

RANGE

Kitchen

REF.

PANTRY

Stor.

STAIRS DN.

Garage
19⁵ x 19⁹

Bath

LIN.

COATS

Bedroom 2
11³ x 11³

Foyer
11'-0" HIGH CEILING

Dining Room
11⁵ x 13³
11'-0" HIGH CEILING

STAIRS UP

Laund.

W.

D.

copyright © 2002 frank betz associates, inc.

*Main floor*

Covered Porch

Attic

Opt. Bath

Opt. Bed. 4
11¹⁰ x 14²

STAIRS DN.

*Optional second floor*

Bedrooms 4
Baths 3
Width 62'-0"
Depth 51'-10"
Main Level 1769 sq ft
Total Living Area 1769 sq ft
Opt. 2nd Floor 289 sq ft

# New Albany

Plan Number: MLFB04-1236
Price Code: D

*From the Southern Living® Design Collection* - This quaint one-story design combines classic architectural detail with a charming cottage feel. Elegant columns grace the front porch to create an inviting entry, while bright windows and a wide center gable offer a memorable first impression. Inside, the New Albany uses every bit of its 1,920 square feet. Formal living and dining rooms make ideal gathering spaces for a delightful holiday meal or a private library. The family room is marked by an arched opening flanked by columns for a sense of arrival. With twelve-foot ceilings in the dining room, living room and family rooms, the home offers a lofty feel. The expansive master suite features a tray ceiling and bright windows. The master bath is complete with his and her vanities, a vaulted ceiling and spacious walk-in closet. An optional basement stair location adds flexibility and room to grow. ■

Foundations Available: Basement, Crawl or Slab

*Rear elevation*

master bedroom
12'5"×16'9"

family room
15'0"×16'10"

breakfast
11'7"×9'6"

bedroom
12'1"×11'6"

kitchen
11'7"×11'11"

bedroom
11'4"×11'4"

living
11'0"×11'7"

foyer

dining
11'3"×11'2"

garage
19'5"×19'9"

covered porch

*Main floor*

copyright © 1999 frank betz associates, inc.

| | |
|---|---|
| Bedrooms | 3 |
| Baths | 2 |
| Width | 59'-0" |
| Depth | 54'-6" |
| Main Level | 1920 sq ft |
| Total Living Area | 1920 sq ft |

# Guilford

Plan Number: MLFB04-3689
Price Code: D

Quaint…Timeless…Classic… all of these so accurately describe the charm that the Guilford exudes. From the cheery dormers, to the comfy front porch, to the board-and-batten shutters, this design stepped off the streets of yesteryear. Inside, the master suite features a wall of windows with views to the backyard. Two additional bedrooms share a divided bath. Decorative columns surround the dining room, enhancing the space without impeding it. An optional second floor adds 519 square feet to this design, providing an additional bedroom, bathroom and bonus area that can be used as guest quarters, a playroom, media room or home office. ■

Foundations Available: Basement or Crawl

*Rear elevation*

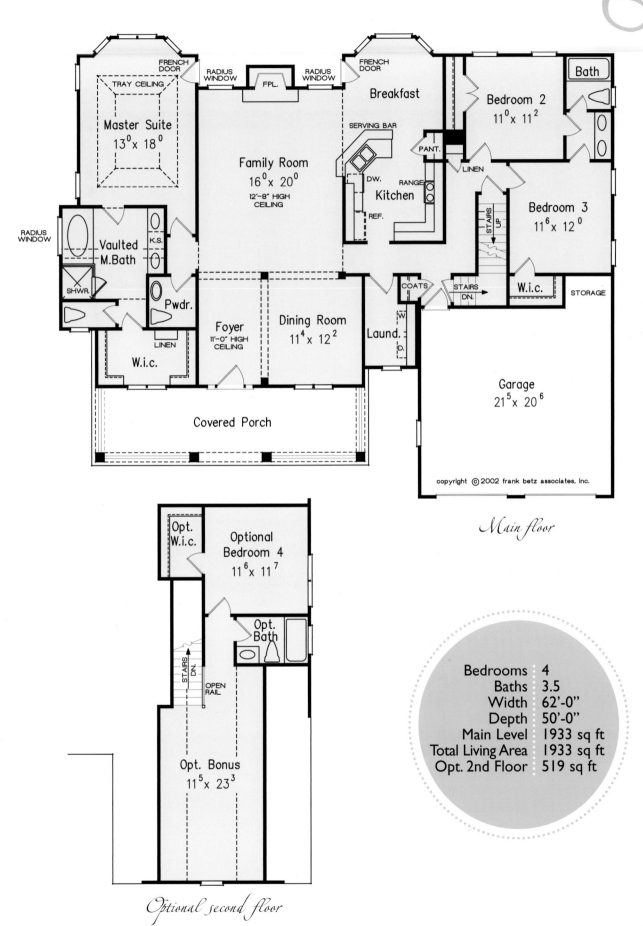

FRENCH DOOR
RADIUS WINDOW
FPL.
RADIUS WINDOW
FRENCH DOOR
Breakfast
Bath
Bedroom 2
$11^0$ x $11^2$

TRAY CEILING
Master Suite
$13^0$ x $18^0$

Family Room
$16^0$ x $20^0$
12'-8" HIGH CEILING

SERVING BAR
DW.
RANGE
Kitchen
REF.

PANT.
LINEN

STAIRS UP

Bedroom 3
$11^6$ x $12^0$

RADIUS WINDOW
Vaulted M.Bath
K.S.

SHWR.
Pwdr.
LINEN
W.i.c.

COATS

STAIRS DN.
W.i.c.
STORAGE

Foyer
11'-0" HIGH CEILING
Dining Room
$11^4$ x $12^2$
Laund.
W
D.

Garage
$21^5$ x $20^6$

Covered Porch

copyright © 2002 frank betz associates, inc.

*Main floor*

Opt. W.i.c.
Optional Bedroom 4
$11^6$ x $11^7$

Opt. Bath

STAIRS DN.
OPEN RAIL

Opt. Bonus
$11^5$ x $23^3$

| | |
|---|---|
| Bedrooms | 4 |
| Baths | 3.5 |
| Width | 62'-0" |
| Depth | 50'-0" |
| Main Level | 1933 sq ft |
| Total Living Area | 1933 sq ft |
| Opt. 2nd Floor | 519 sq ft |

*Optional second floor*

# Delaney

Plan Number: MLFB04-3744
Price Code: D

Symmetry prevails on this brick-and-siding elevation, with refined colonial influences such as twin dormers, fanlight transoms and a paneled door. Curves of the arch-topped windows are repeated in the entry colonnade and in the gable windows. A lovely formal dining room is announced by two decorative columns and a graceful archway. Twin windows permit ample views of the front property. At the center of the plan, radius windows frame a focal-point fireplace in the great room. The breakfast room and kitchen form a spacious, well-lit arena that opens to the outside through a French door. A flex room easily converts from a home office to guest quarters. ■

Foundations Available: Basement or Crawl

*Rear elevation*

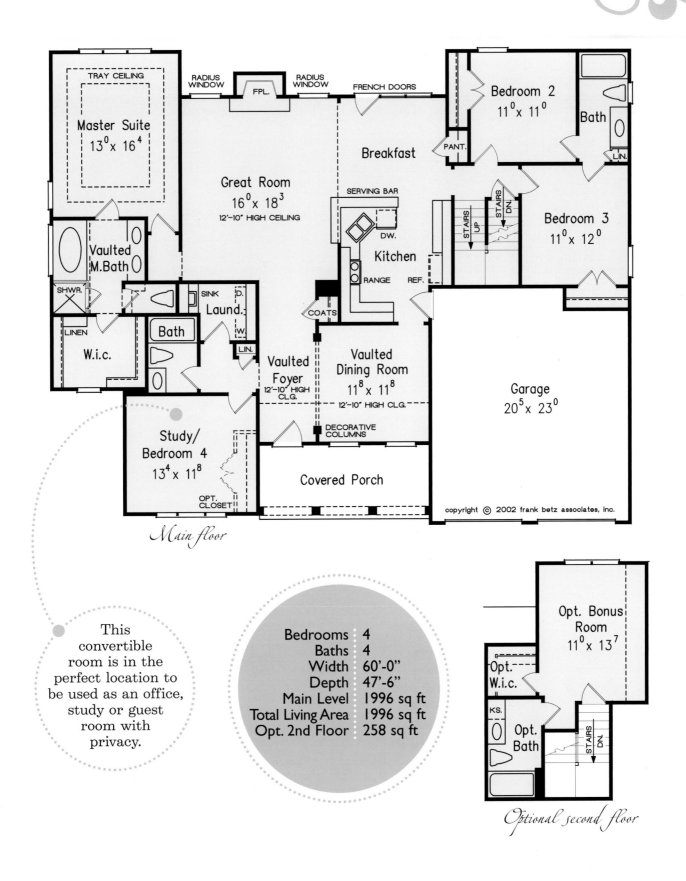

TRAY CEILING

RADIUS WINDOW    FPL.    RADIUS WINDOW    FRENCH DOORS

Master Suite
13⁰ x 16⁴

Great Room
16⁰ x 18³
12'-10" HIGH CEILING

Breakfast

Bedroom 2
11⁰ x 11⁰

Bath

PANT.

SERVING BAR

Vaulted M.Bath

DW.

Kitchen

RANGE    REF.

STAIRS UP    STAIRS DN.

Bedroom 3
11⁰ x 12⁰

SHWR.

LINEN

W.i.c.

SINK    D.
Laund.    W.

Bath    LIN.

COATS

Vaulted Foyer
12'-10" HIGH CLG.

Vaulted Dining Room
11⁸ x 11⁸
12'-10" HIGH CLG.

Garage
20⁵ x 23⁰

Study/ Bedroom 4
13⁴ x 11⁸

OPT. CLOSET

DECORATIVE COLUMNS

Covered Porch

copyright © 2002 frank betz associates, inc.

*Main floor*

This convertible room is in the perfect location to be used as an office, study or guest room with privacy.

| | |
|---|---|
| Bedrooms | 4 |
| Baths | 4 |
| Width | 60'-0" |
| Depth | 47'-6" |
| Main Level | 1996 sq ft |
| Total Living Area | 1996 sq ft |
| Opt. 2nd Floor | 258 sq ft |

Opt. Bonus Room
11⁰ x 13⁷

Opt. W.i.c.

KS.

Opt. Bath

STAIRS DN.

*Optional second floor*

# Seabrooke

Plan Number: MLFB04-3842
Price Code: D

The Seabrooke exhibits curb appeal that is a welcome addition to any street or neighborhood. Its warm combination of fieldstone, dormers and board-and-batten shutters sends a message of friendliness and congeniality. Modern design features inside make this house as family-friendly as it is charming. A vaulted keeping room is situated just off the kitchen area, giving families a comfortable place to spend casual time together. Decorative columns surround the dining room, serving as a subtle divider from the rest of the home. The master suite earns its name with its own private sitting area. Optional bonus space is available that gives room for expansion to use as you wish. ▪

Foundations Available: Basement, Crawl or Slab

*Rear elevation*

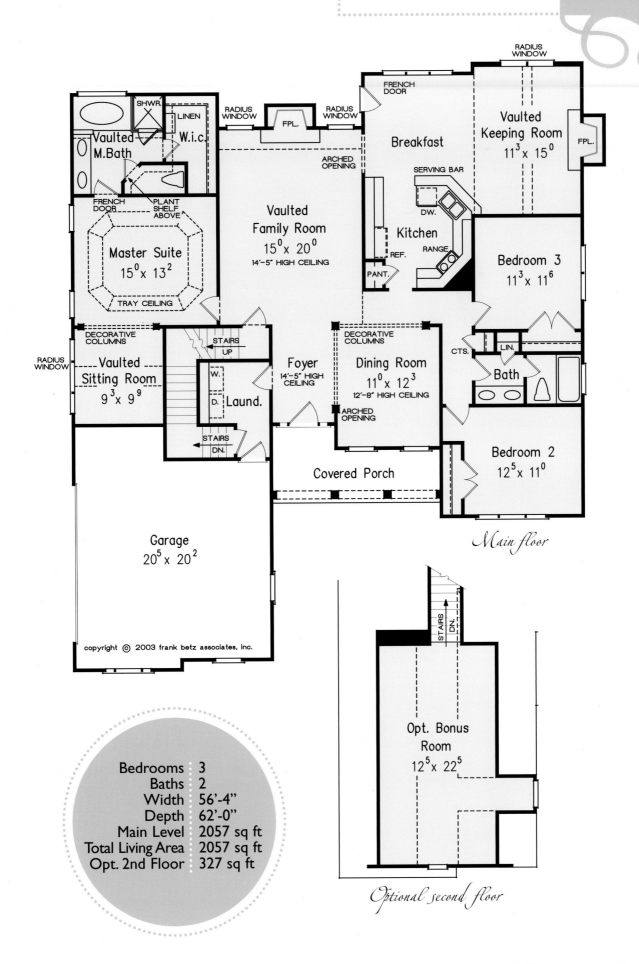

SHWR.

LINEN

Vaulted M.Bath

W.i.c.

RADIUS WINDOW

FPL.

RADIUS WINDOW

FRENCH DOOR

RADIUS WINDOW

Breakfast

Vaulted Keeping Room
$11^3$ x $15^0$

FPL.

FRENCH DOOR

PLANT SHELF ABOVE

Master Suite
$15^0$ x $13^2$

TRAY CEILING

Vaulted Family Room
$15^0$ x $20^0$
14'-5" HIGH CEILING

ARCHED OPENING

SERVING BAR

Kitchen

DW.

REF.

RANGE

PANT.

Bedroom 3
$11^3$ x $11^6$

DECORATIVE COLUMNS

RADIUS WINDOW

Vaulted Sitting Room
$9^3$ x $9^9$

STAIRS UP

W.

D.

Laund.

Foyer
14'-5" HIGH CEILING

DECORATIVE COLUMNS

Dining Room
$11^0$ x $12^3$
12'-8" HIGH CEILING

CTS.

LIN.

Bath

STAIRS DN.

ARCHED OPENING

Bedroom 2
$12^5$ x $11^0$

Covered Porch

Garage
$20^5$ x $20^2$

*Main floor*

copyright © 2003 frank betz associates, inc.

STAIRS DN.

Opt. Bonus Room
$12^5$ x $22^5$

*Optional second floor*

| | |
|---|---|
| Bedrooms | 3 |
| Baths | 2 |
| Width | 56'-4" |
| Depth | 62'-0" |
| Main Level | 2057 sq ft |
| Total Living Area | 2057 sq ft |
| Opt. 2nd Floor | 327 sq ft |

# Colemans Bluff

Plan Number: MLFB04-3896
Price Code: D

Exterior materials that complement one another are the key to an attractive elevation. On the Colemans Bluff, the stone, cedar shake, and carriage garage doors come together to create a façade that is warm and street friendly. Its floor plan is just as inviting, with a coffered ceiling providing a unique canopy over the family room. A large screened porch off the breakfast area provides the perfect spot for outdoor living. The garage entry filters traffic through the mudroom, which is fully equipped with a coat closet, bench, wall hooks and access to the laundry room. Finishing the optional second floor adds a bedroom, bath and bonus room to the design. ■

Foundations Available: Basement or Crawl

*Rear elevation*

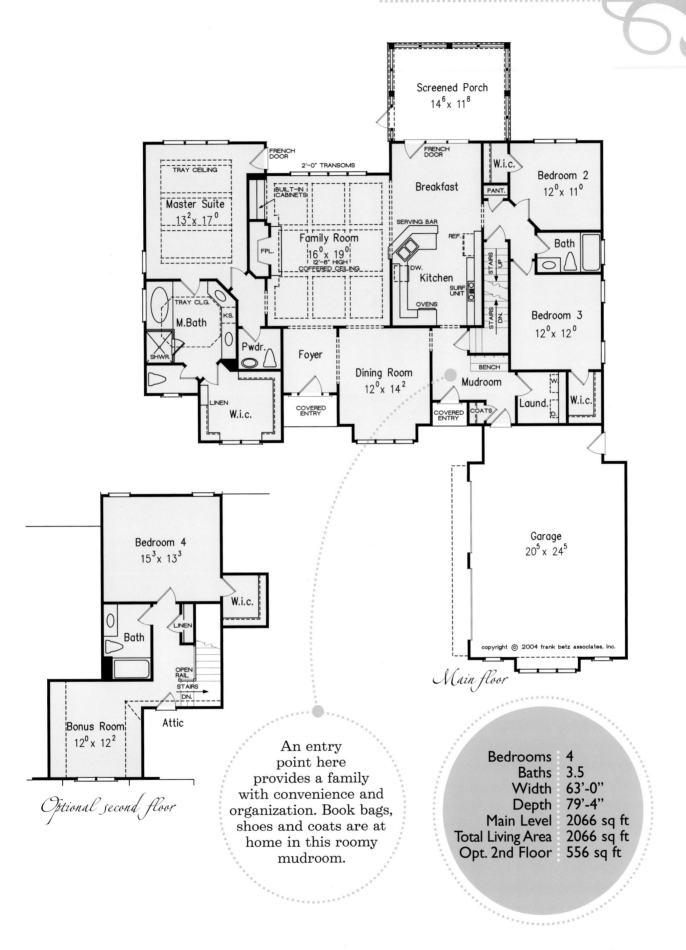

Screened Porch
$14^6$ x $11^8$

TRAY CEILING

Master Suite
$13^2$ x $17^0$

FRENCH DOOR

2'-0" TRANSOMS

BUILT-IN CABINETS

FPL.

Family Room
$16^0$ x $19^0$
12'-6" HIGH COFFERED CEILING

FRENCH DOOR

Breakfast

W.i.c.

PANT.

Bedroom 2
$12^0$ x $11^0$

SERVING BAR

REF.

DW.

Kitchen

SURF. UNIT

OVENS

STAIRS UP

STAIRS DN.

Bath

TRAY CLG.

M.Bath

KS.

SHWR.

Pwdr.

Foyer

Dining Room
$12^0$ x $14^2$

Mudroom

BENCH

Bedroom 3
$12^0$ x $12^0$

LINEN

W.i.c.

COVERED ENTRY

COVERED ENTRY

COATS

Laund.

W
D.

W.i.c.

Garage
$20^5$ x $24^5$

copyright © 2004 frank betz associates, inc.

*Main floor*

Bedroom 4
$15^3$ x $13^3$

W.i.c.

Bath

LINEN

OPEN RAIL STAIRS DN.

Bonus Room
$12^0$ x $12^2$

Attic

*Optional second floor*

An entry point here provides a family with convenience and organization. Book bags, shoes and coats are at home in this roomy mudroom.

| | |
|---|---|
| Bedrooms | 4 |
| Baths | 3.5 |
| Width | 63'-0" |
| Depth | 79'-4" |
| Main Level | 2066 sq ft |
| Total Living Area | 2066 sq ft |
| Opt. 2nd Floor | 556 sq ft |

# Walnut Grove

Plan Number: MLFB04-3865
Price Code: D

This design was created for the homeowner who wants upscale features on one level. Its cozy fieldstone exterior sets the stage for an equally impressive design inside. Two separate living spaces — the keeping and family rooms — give residents and guests alike options on where to gather. Double ovens and a serving bar in the kitchen make meal preparation and entertaining fun and easy. A covered porch is accessed from the breakfast area, giving homeowners a quiet and peaceful spot to unwind. The master suite is private from the other bedrooms, and features a tray ceiling, a corner soaking tub and serene backyard views. ■

Foundations Available: Basement or Crawl

*Rear elevation*

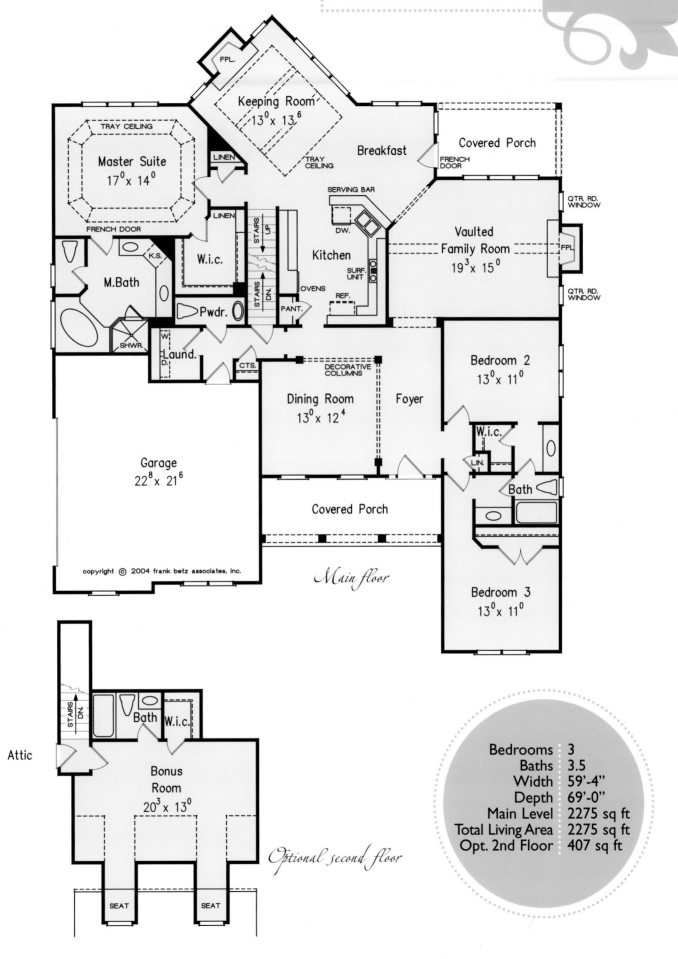

FPL.

Keeping Room
13⁰ x 13.⁶

TRAY CEILING

Master Suite
17⁰ x 14⁰

TRAY CEILING

LINEN

Breakfast

Covered Porch

FRENCH DOOR

LINEN

W.i.c.

STAIRS UP

SERVING BAR

DW.

Vaulted
Family Room
19³ x 15⁰

QTR. RD. WINDOW

FPL

K.S.

M.Bath

STAIRS DN.

Kitchen

SURF. UNIT

OVENS

REF.

QTR. RD. WINDOW

Pwdr.

PANT.

W.

D.

SHWR.

Laund.

CTS.

DECORATIVE COLUMNS

Dining Room
13⁰ x 12⁴

Foyer

Bedroom 2
13⁰ x 11⁰

W.i.c.

LIN.

Bath

Garage
22⁸ x 21⁶

copyright © 2004 frank betz associates, inc.

Covered Porch

*Main floor*

Bedroom 3
13⁰ x 11⁰

STAIRS DN.

Bath

W.i.c.

Attic

Bonus
Room
20³ x 13⁰

SEAT

SEAT

*Optional second floor*

| | |
|---|---|
| Bedrooms | 3 |
| Baths | 3.5 |
| Width | 59'-4" |
| Depth | 69'-0" |
| Main Level | 2275 sq ft |
| Total Living Area | 2275 sq ft |
| Opt. 2nd Floor | 407 sq ft |

# Kingsport

Plan Number: MLFB04-3745
Price Code: E

Clapboard siding and carriage garage doors create that cottage appeal that so many of today's homeowners are in search of. The Kingsport is as warm and welcoming inside as it is outside. The kitchen area is bright and cheery with a bay window in the breakfast area. This space caters to casual family time with a cozy keeping room connected to it. Transom windows in the breakfast and keeping rooms allow the extra light to pour in. An optional second floor provides the opportunity for a fourth bedroom, as well as additional space ideal for a customized playroom, craft room or exercise area. ■

Foundations Available: Basement, Crawl or Slab

*Rear elevation*

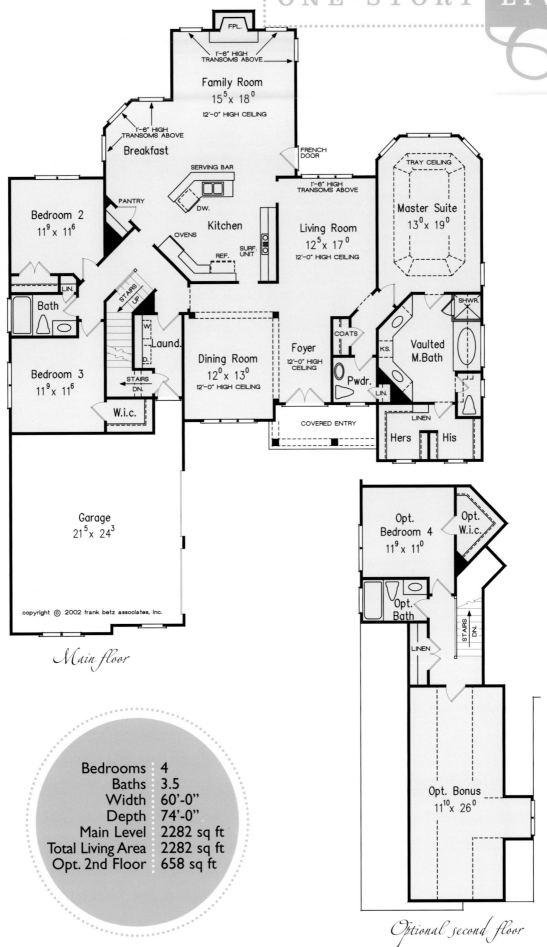

FPL.

Family Room
15⁵ x 18⁰
12'-0" HIGH CEILING

1'-6" HIGH
TRANSOMS ABOVE

1'-6" HIGH
TRANSOMS ABOVE

Breakfast

SERVING BAR

DW.

Kitchen

OVENS

REF.

SURF.
UNIT

FRENCH
DOOR

1'-6" HIGH
TRANSOMS ABOVE

Living Room
12⁵ x 17⁰
12'-0" HIGH CEILING

Master Suite
13⁰ x 19⁰

TRAY CEILING

SHWR.

PANTRY

Bedroom 2
11⁹ x 11⁶

LIN.

Bath

STAIRS
UP

W.

D.

Laund.

Bedroom 3
11⁹ x 11⁶

STAIRS
DN.

W.i.c.

Dining Room
12⁰ x 13⁰
12'-0" HIGH CEILING

Foyer
12'-0" HIGH
CEILING

COATS

Pwdr.

LIN.

COVERED ENTRY

Vaulted
M.Bath

K.S.

LINEN

Hers

His

LINEN

Garage
21⁵ x 24³

copyright © 2002 frank betz associates, inc.

*Main floor*

Opt.
Bedroom 4
11⁹ x 11⁰

Opt.
W.i.c.

Opt.
Bath

STAIRS
DN.

LINEN

Opt. Bonus
11¹⁰ x 26⁰

*Optional second floor*

Bedrooms | 4
Baths | 3.5
Width | 60'-0"
Depth | 74'-0"
Main Level | 2282 sq ft
Total Living Area | 2282 sq ft
Opt. 2nd Floor | 658 sq ft

# Cassidy

Plan Number: MLFB04-969
Price Code: E

Stately brick and European stucco are a likely and familiar combination that creates Old World charm. A smart and functional split-bedroom design, the Cassidy is made extra special in its details. The master suite has a private sitting area with a fireplace that gives owners a peaceful place to spend time reading or relaxing. A vaulted ceiling keeps the breakfast room feeling open and bright. Decorating just got easier with plant shelves, arched openings and decorative columns placed throughout the home. The laundry room, a coat closet and a powder room are all situated near the garage entry adding convenience for the entire family. ◼

Foundations Available: Basement, Crawl or Slab

*Rear elevation*

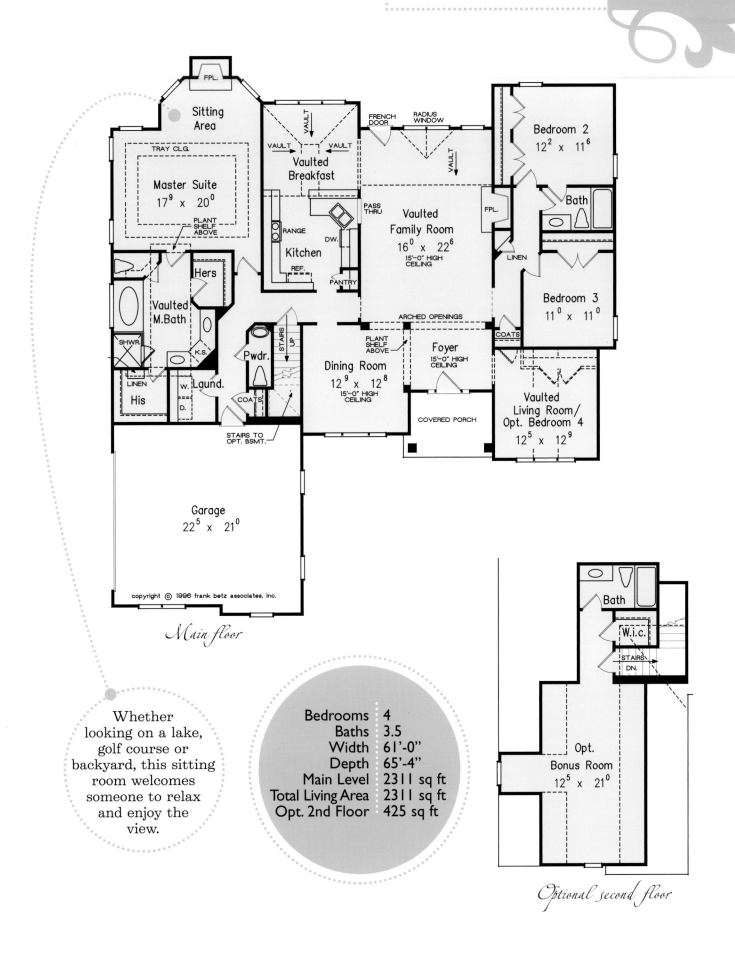

*Main floor*

*Optional second floor*

Whether looking on a lake, golf course or backyard, this sitting room welcomes someone to relax and enjoy the view.

| | |
|---|---|
| Bedrooms | 4 |
| Baths | 3.5 |
| Width | 61'-0" |
| Depth | 65'-4" |
| Main Level | 2311 sq ft |
| Total Living Area | 2311 sq ft |
| Opt. 2nd Floor | 425 sq ft |

© 1999 Frank Betz Associates, Inc.

# Sanderson Place

Plan Number: MLFB04-1250
Price Code: F

Not many home plans offer this much house on one level. *From the Southern Living® Design Collection*, Sanderson Place captures the spirit of "home" distinguished by beautiful rooflines and fully efficient, modern floor plan. This plan is ideal for a family, especially one that prefers multiple spaces working together as a unit. It features a family room that opens from the foyer and provides a central link for the kitchen, breakfast room and dining room. Cased openings and hallways connect private sections of the house to the living areas, minimizing noise. Its split-bedroom design secludes the master suite from the other bedrooms. A functional utility room is located just off the garage. ■

Foundations Available: Basement, Crawl or Slab

*Rear elevation*

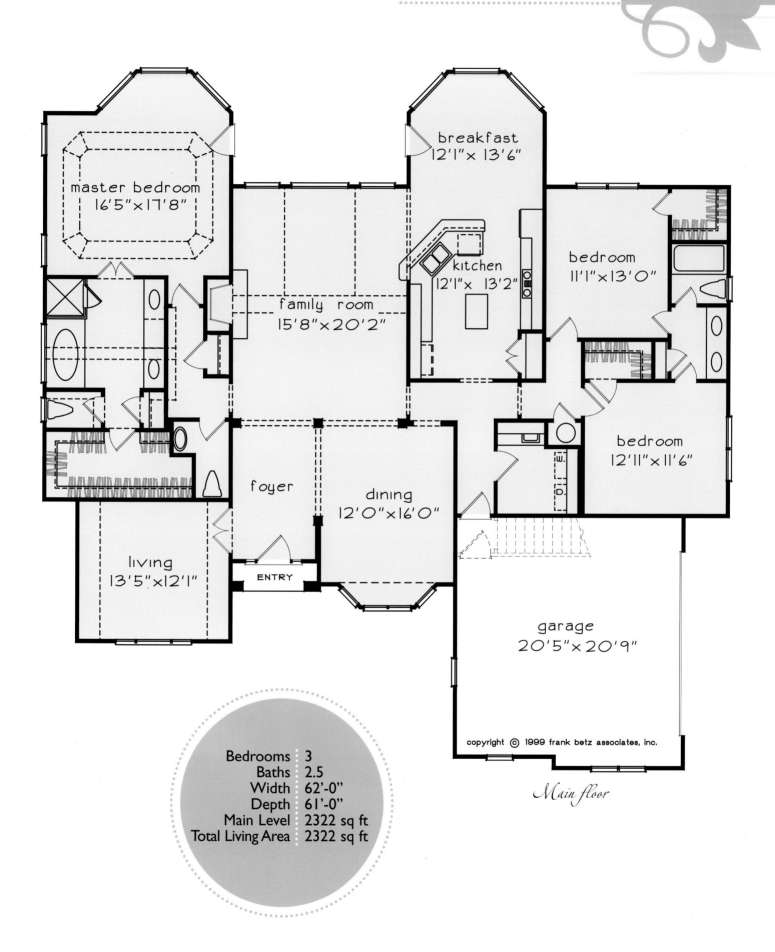

master bedroom
16'5"×17'8"

breakfast
12'1"×13'6"

kitchen
12'1"×13'2"

bedroom
11'1"×13'0"

family room
15'8"×20'2"

bedroom
12'11"×11'6"

foyer

dining
12'0"×16'0"

living
13'5"×12'1"

ENTRY

garage
20'5"×20'9"

copyright © 1999 frank betz associates, inc.

*Main floor*

| | |
|---|---|
| Bedrooms | 3 |
| Baths | 2.5 |
| Width | 62'-0" |
| Depth | 61'-0" |
| Main Level | 2322 sq ft |
| Total Living Area | 2322 sq ft |

# Northbrook

Plan Number: MLFB04-3625
Price Code: D

The Northbrook just looks like a place you'd call "home" with its stone exterior and board-and-batten shutters. Family time is well spent in the adjoining breakfast area and keeping room. Decorative columns and transom windows accent the grand room, making the perfect spot for parties or family gatherings. A built-in desk has been incorporated into the kitchen area keeping things neat and organized. The master suite is discreetly located to allow for privacy. The optional bedroom and bath are located upstairs for future expansion. ▪

Foundations Available: Basement or Crawl

*Rear elevation*

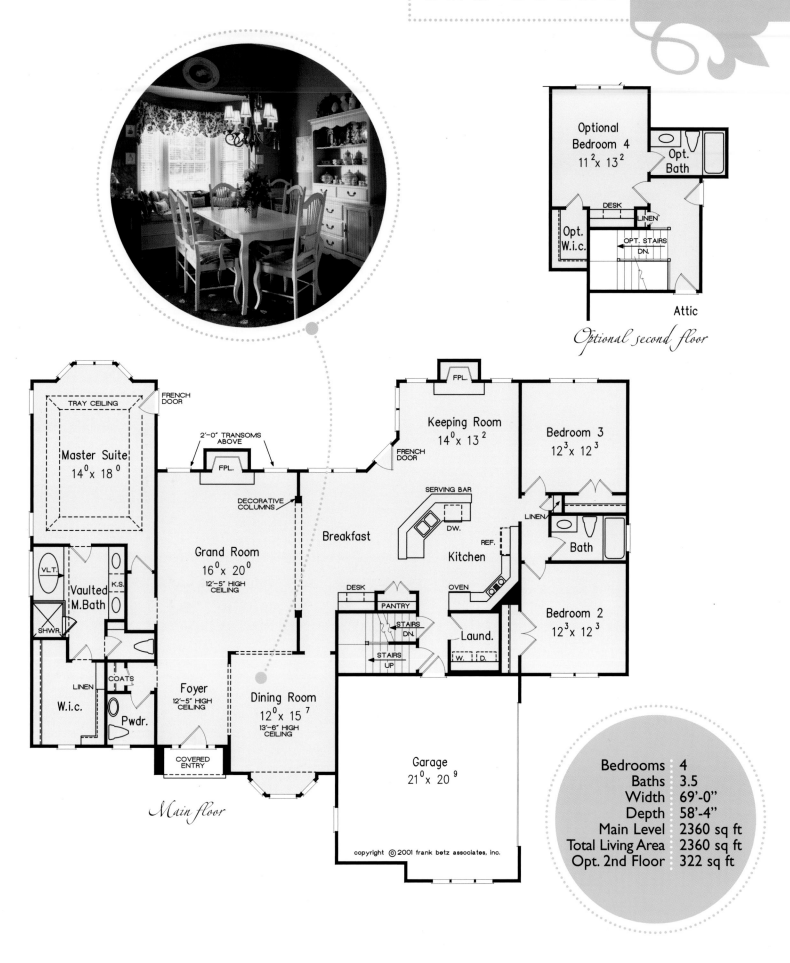

Optional
Bedroom 4
$11^2$ x $13^2$

Opt.
Bath

DESK

LINEN

Opt.
W.i.c.

OPT. STAIRS
DN.

Attic

*Optional second floor*

FRENCH
DOOR

TRAY CEILING

Master Suite
$14^0$ x $18^0$

2'-0" TRANSOMS
ABOVE

FPL.

DECORATIVE
COLUMNS

FPL.

Keeping Room
$14^0$ x $13^2$

FRENCH
DOOR

Bedroom 3
$12^3$ x $12^3$

VLT.

Vaulted
M.Bath

K.S.

SHWR.

Grand Room
$16^0$ x $20^0$
12'-5" HIGH
CEILING

Breakfast

SERVING BAR

DW.

Kitchen

REF.

LINEN

Bath

LINEN

COATS

W.i.c.

Pwdr.

Foyer
12'-5" HIGH
CEILING

Dining Room
$12^0$ x $15^7$
13'-6" HIGH
CEILING

COVERED
ENTRY

DESK

PANTRY

STAIRS
DN.

STAIRS
UP

OVEN

Laund.

W. D.

Bedroom 2
$12^3$ x $12^3$

Garage
$21^0$ x $20^9$

*Main floor*

copyright © 2001 frank betz associates, inc.

| | |
|---|---|
| Bedrooms | 4 |
| Baths | 3.5 |
| Width | 69'-0" |
| Depth | 58'-4" |
| Main Level | 2360 sq ft |
| Total Living Area | 2360 sq ft |
| Opt. 2nd Floor | 322 sq ft |

# Camden Lake

Plan Number: MLFB04-3828
Price Code: E

One glance will tell you that this home is original and unique in its design and details. Beamed gables and cedar shake create an appealing Craftsman-style elevation. The pleasant surprises keep coming inside where entertainers will fall in love with this floor plan! The kitchen is adorned with many added extras that make it a fun place to be. Double ovens, a serving bar and a liberally sized pantry make it a user-friendly room. Its view to the cozy keeping room warms the entire space, creating an inviting environment. Built-in cabinetry in the family room provides plenty of storage, as well as unique spaces to decorate. Arched openings and decorative columns add originality to the design. ∎

Foundations Available: Basement or Crawl

*Rear elevation*

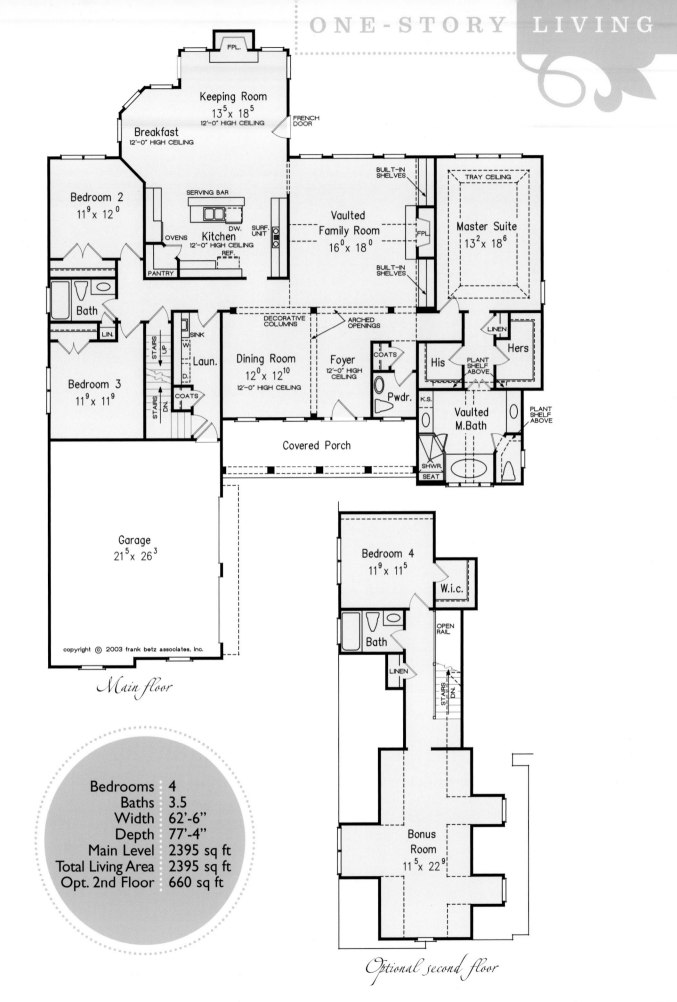

FPL.

Keeping Room
13⁵ x 18⁵
12'-0" HIGH CEILING

FRENCH DOOR

Breakfast
12'-0" HIGH CEILING

Bedroom 2
11⁹ x 12⁰

SERVING BAR

DW.

SURF. UNIT

OVENS

Kitchen
12'-0" HIGH CEILING

REF.

PANTRY

Bath

LIN.

Vaulted Family Room
16⁰ x 18⁰

BUILT-IN SHELVES

BUILT-IN SHELVES

FPL

TRAY CEILING

Master Suite
13² x 18⁶

LINEN

Hers

His

PLANT SHELF ABOVE

PLANT SHELF ABOVE

STAIRS UP

Laun.

SINK

W

D

COATS

STAIRS DN.

Bedroom 3
11⁹ x 11⁹

DECORATIVE COLUMNS

ARCHED OPENINGS

Dining Room
12⁰ x 12¹⁰
12'-0" HIGH CEILING

Foyer
12'-0" HIGH CEILING

COATS

Pwdr.

K.S.

Vaulted M.Bath

SHWR.

SEAT

Covered Porch

Garage
21⁵ x 26³

copyright © 2003 frank betz associates, inc.

*Main floor*

Bedroom 4
11⁹ x 11⁵

W.i.c.

Bath

LINEN

OPEN RAIL

STAIRS DN.

Bonus Room
11⁵ x 22⁹

*Optional second floor*

| | |
|---|---|
| Bedrooms | 4 |
| Baths | 3.5 |
| Width | 62'-6" |
| Depth | 77'-4" |
| Main Level | 2395 sq ft |
| Total Living Area | 2395 sq ft |
| Opt. 2nd Floor | 660 sq ft |

# Blackstone

Plan Number: MLFB04-3871
Price Code: E

*From the Southern Living® Design Collection* - Craftsman-styled homes are increasing in popularity because of their welcoming blends of exterior materials. Cedar shake and stacked stone accent the board-and-batten siding on the façade of the Blackstone to create a friendly curb appeal. Careful design details inside are equally as impressive. A vaulted master suite is divided from the other bedrooms, making a private haven for homeowners to enjoy. The breakfast area leads to a screened porch and oversized deck on the back of the home — perfect for outdoor entertaining. A mudroom buffers the living area from the garage, ensuring that coats and shoes stay in their place. The second and third bedrooms share a divided bath, with double sinks separate from the bathing area. ■

Foundations Available: Basement or Crawl

*Rear elevation*

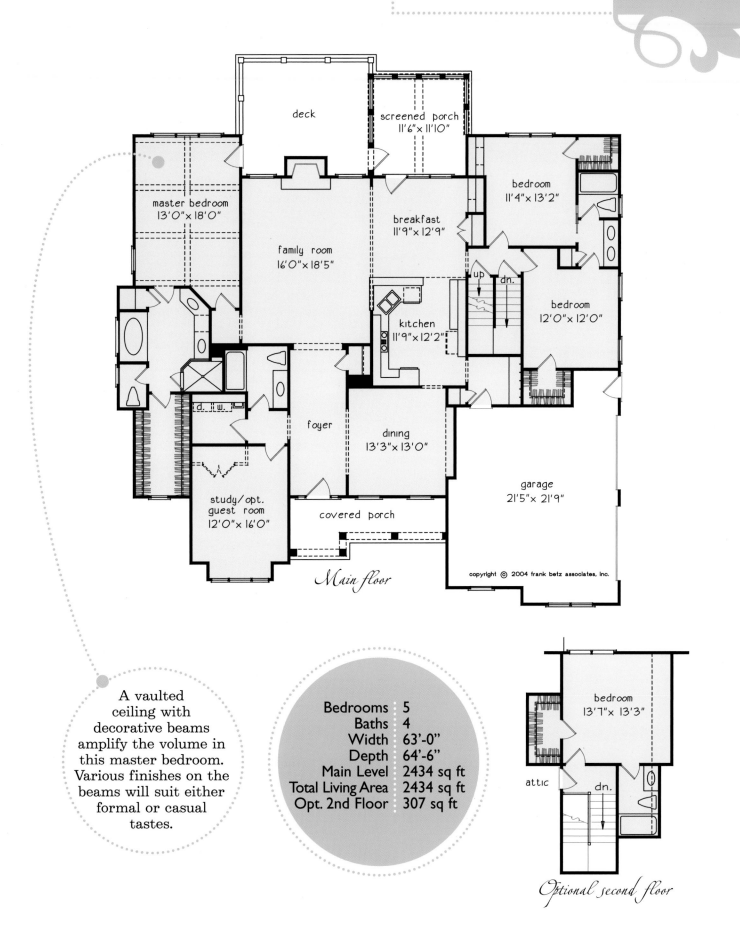

deck

screened porch
11'6" x 11'10"

master bedroom
13'0" x 18'0"

bedroom
11'4" x 13'2"

family room
16'0" x 18'5"

breakfast
11'9" x 12'9"

up    dn.

bedroom
12'0" x 12'0"

kitchen
11'9" x 12'2"

d. w.

foyer

dining
13'3" x 13'0"

garage
21'5" x 21'9"

study/opt.
guest room
12'0" x 16'0"

covered porch

copyright © 2004 frank betz associates, inc.

*Main floor*

A vaulted
ceiling with
decorative beams
amplify the volume in
this master bedroom.
Various finishes on the
beams will suit either
formal or casual
tastes.

| | |
|---|---|
| Bedrooms | 5 |
| Baths | 4 |
| Width | 63'-0" |
| Depth | 64'-6" |
| Main Level | 2434 sq ft |
| Total Living Area | 2434 sq ft |
| Opt. 2nd Floor | 307 sq ft |

bedroom
13'7" x 13'3"

attic

dn.

*Optional second floor*

# Devonhurst

Plan Number: MLFB04-3806
Price Code: E

Bring the rocking chairs – your front porch awaits you! Columns enhance this rocking-chair front porch and create a relaxing end-of-the-day retreat! Stepping inside you'll find a very open, unobstructed floor plan. The dining room is bordered by decorative columns, allowing effortless flow to the other living areas. The breakfast area and keeping room share open access to the kitchen – perfect for family gathering or parties. High ceilings always enhance the volume of a home, so vaults were incorporated into the keeping and family rooms. An optional second floor is available, adding another bedroom and a large children's retreat to the design. ■

Foundations Available: Basement or Crawl

*Rear elevation*

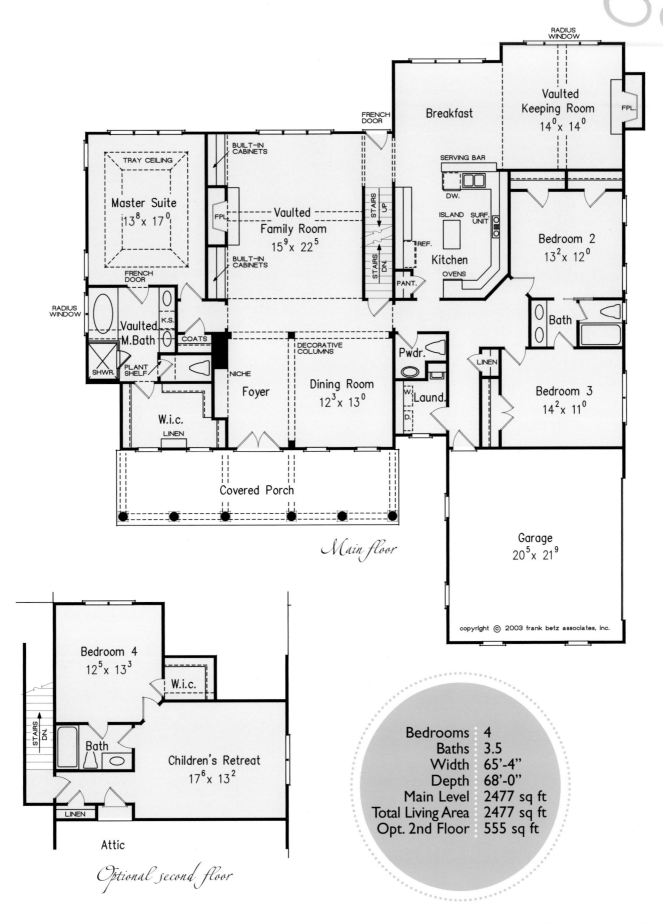

TRAY CEILING

Master Suite
13⁸ x 17⁰

BUILT-IN CABINETS

Vaulted Family Room
15⁹ x 22⁵

FRENCH DOOR

Breakfast

Vaulted Keeping Room
14⁰ x 14⁰

FPL.

RADIUS WINDOW

FPL.

STAIRS UP

STAIRS DN

SERVING BAR

DW.

ISLAND

SURF. UNIT

OVENS

Kitchen

REF.

PANT.

BUILT-IN CABINETS

Bedroom 2
13² x 12⁰

FRENCH DOOR

RADIUS WINDOW

Vaulted M.Bath

K.S.

COATS

SHWR.

PLANT SHELF

Bath

LINEN

NICHE

Foyer

Dining Room
12³ x 13⁰

DECORATIVE COLUMNS

Pwdr.

Laund.

W. D.

Bedroom 3
14² x 11⁰

W.i.c.

LINEN

Covered Porch

*Main floor*

Garage
20⁵ x 21⁹

copyright © 2003 frank betz associates, inc.

Bedroom 4
12⁵ x 13³

W.i.c.

STAIRS DN.

Bath

Children's Retreat
17⁶ x 13²

LINEN

Attic

*Optional second floor*

| | |
|---|---|
| Bedrooms | 4 |
| Baths | 3.5 |
| Width | 65'-4" |
| Depth | 68'-0" |
| Main Level | 2477 sq ft |
| Total Living Area | 2477 sq ft |
| Opt. 2nd Floor | 555 sq ft |

# Finley

Plan Number: MLFB04-903
Price Code: E

The classy and upscale appeal of European stucco will never go out of style. Embellished with fieldstone accents, the Finley's façade is as welcoming as it is eye-catching. But the real treat is inside...with a floor plan that is sure to please! The master suite was designed to be a true haven for its resident. Its private sitting room is an extension of the suite, with dimensions generous enough to house plenty of furniture or exercise equipment. Unlike many of its one-level counterparts, the Finley has two living rooms: one serving as the home's focal point and one adjoining the breakfast area for informal gatherings. ▪

Foundations Available: Basement, Crawl or Slab

*Rear elevation*

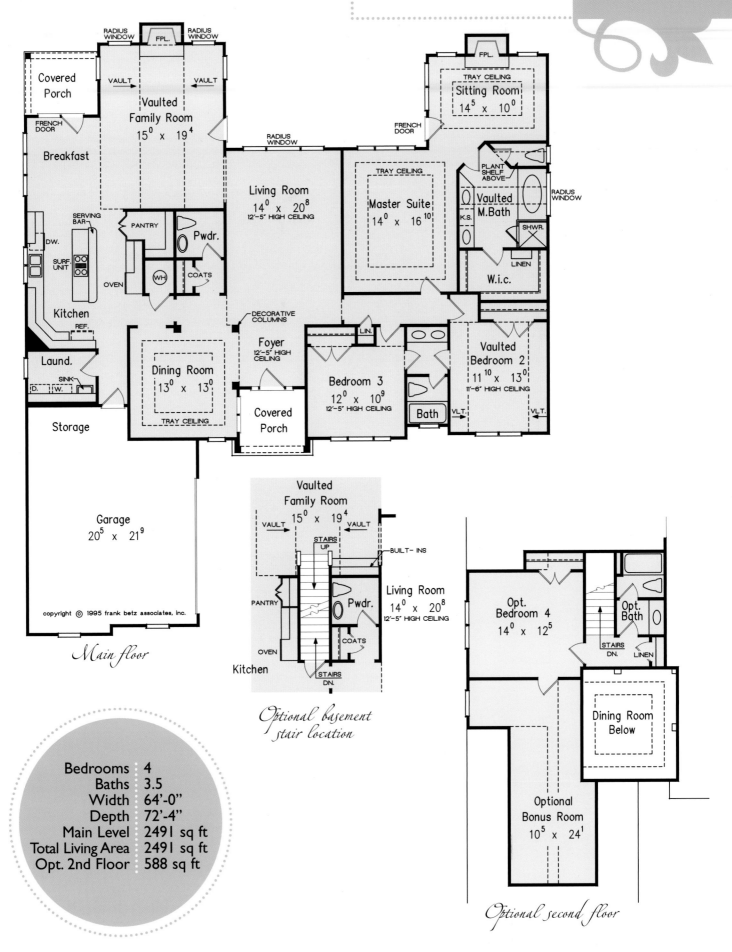

RADIUS WINDOW · FPL. · RADIUS WINDOW

Covered Porch

VAULT · VAULT

Vaulted Family Room
15⁰ x 19⁴

FRENCH DOOR

Breakfast

SERVING BAR

PANTRY

Pwdr.

DW.

SURF. UNIT

OVEN · WH · COATS

Kitchen

REF.

Laund.

SINK · D. · W.

Storage

Garage
20⁵ x 21⁹

copyright © 1995 frank betz associates, inc.

*Main floor*

RADIUS WINDOW

Living Room
14⁰ x 20⁸
12'-5" HIGH CEILING

DECORATIVE COLUMNS

Foyer
12'-5" HIGH CEILING

Covered Porch

Dining Room
13⁰ x 13⁰
TRAY CEILING

TRAY CEILING

Master Suite
14⁰ x 16¹⁰

FRENCH DOOR

TRAY CEILING
Sitting Room
14⁵ x 10⁰

FPL.

PLANT SHELF ABOVE

Vaulted M.Bath

K.S. · SHWR. · RADIUS WINDOW

LINEN

W.i.c.

LIN.

Bedroom 3
12⁰ x 10⁹
12'-5" HIGH CEILING

Bath

VLT.

Vaulted Bedroom 2
11¹⁰ x 13⁰
11'-6" HIGH CEILING

VLT.

Vaulted Family Room
15⁰ x 19⁴

VAULT · VAULT

STAIRS UP

BUILT-INS

PANTRY

Pwdr.

OVEN · COATS

Living Room
14⁰ x 20⁸
12'-5" HIGH CEILING

Kitchen

STAIRS DN.

*Optional basement stair location*

Opt. Bedroom 4
14⁰ x 12⁵

Opt. Bath

STAIRS DN. · LINEN

Dining Room Below

Optional Bonus Room
10⁵ x 24¹

*Optional second floor*

Bedrooms : 4
Baths : 3.5
Width : 64'-0"
Depth : 72'-4"
Main Level : 2491 sq ft
Total Living Area : 2491 sq ft
Opt. 2nd Floor : 588 sq ft

# Hennefield

Plan Number: MLFB04-3835
Price Code: E

Timber-accented gables and board-and-batten shutters create a friendly and casual curb appeal that is so desired today. This one-level design is equipped with several added extras that make it original and unique. Just off the kitchen is a vaulted keeping room that is bright and comfortable with radius windows that allow the natural light to illuminate the room. Built-in cabinetry in the family room gives this area an appealing focal point, as well as ample storage and decorating opportunities. The master suite is private from the other bedrooms, and has an enormous closet, divided by a dressing mirror into his-and-hers sections. An optional second floor leaves plenty of room to grow. ■

Foundations Available: Basement, Crawl or Slab

*Rear elevation*

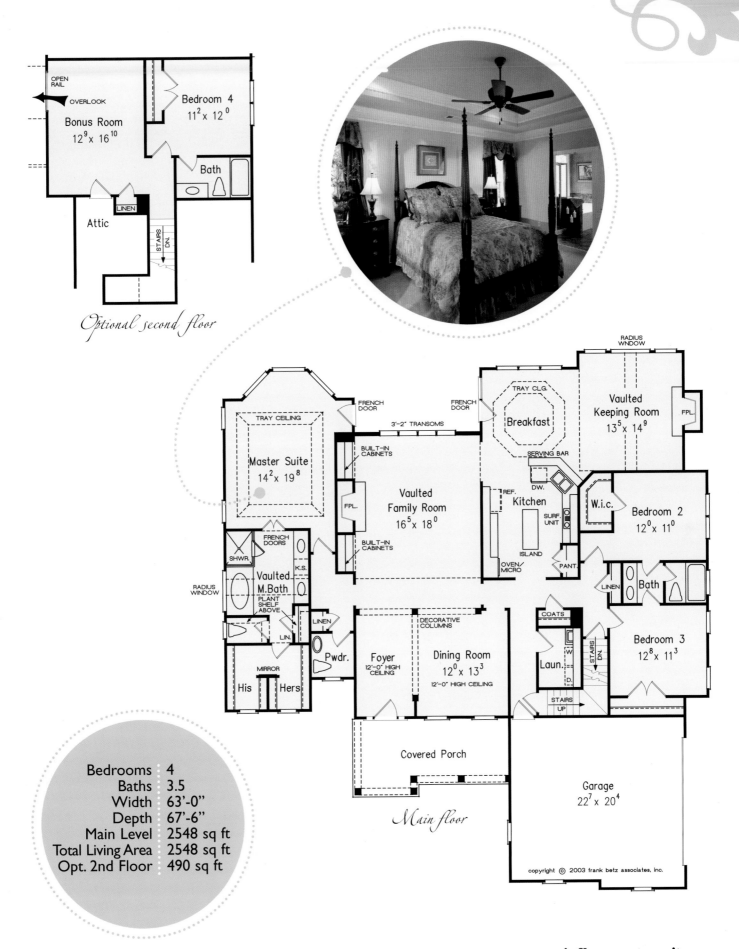

OPEN RAIL

OVERLOOK

Bedroom 4
$11^2$ x $12^0$

Bonus Room
$12^9$ x $16^{10}$

Bath

LINEN

Attic

STAIRS DN.

*Optional second floor*

TRAY CEILING

Master Suite
$14^2$ x $19^8$

FRENCH DOOR

FRENCH DOOR

RADIUS WINDOW

TRAY CLG.

Breakfast

Vaulted Keeping Room
$13^5$ x $14^9$

FPL.

BUILT-IN CABINETS

$3'-2"$ TRANSOMS

SERVING BAR

REF.

DW.

W.i.c.

FPL.

Vaulted Family Room
$16^5$ x $18^0$

Kitchen

Bedroom 2
$12^0$ x $11^0$

SHWR.

FRENCH DOORS

Vaulted M.Bath

K.S.

BUILT-IN CABINETS

SURF. UNIT

ISLAND

LINEN

Bath

RADIUS WINDOW

PLANT SHELF ABOVE

LINEN

LIN.

OVEN/ MICRO

PANT.

COATS

Bedroom 3
$12^8$ x $11^3$

MIRROR

His

Hers

Pwdr.

Foyer
$12'-0"$ HIGH CEILING

DECORATIVE COLUMNS

Dining Room
$12^0$ x $13^3$
$12'-0"$ HIGH CEILING

W

Laun.

D.

STAIRS DN.

STAIRS UP

Covered Porch

Garage
$22^7$ x $20^4$

*Main floor*

copyright © 2003 frank betz associates, inc.

Bedrooms | 4
Baths | 3.5
Width | 63'-0"
Depth | 67'-6"
Main Level | 2548 sq ft
Total Living Area | 2548 sq ft
Opt. 2nd Floor | 490 sq ft

# Nordstrom

Plan Number: MLFB04-3561
Price Code: F

An age-old turret with eye-catching radius windows is the focal point of this not-so-traditional ranch design. Although the façade of the Nordstrom is quite traditional, today's latest and greatest design trends are waiting inside. A massive family room is especially unique with a coffered ceiling, built-in cabinets and backdrop of radius windows. The kitchen adjoins a vaulted keeping room with a fireplace — a comfortable place to relax for the evening. Everyone's needs are a bit different, so flexible spaces have been carefully incorporated. The formal living room can be easily converted into a sitting area for the master bedroom. Upstairs, an optional bedroom and bath make the perfect guest suite or home office. ∎

Foundations Available: Basement or Crawl

*Rear elevation*

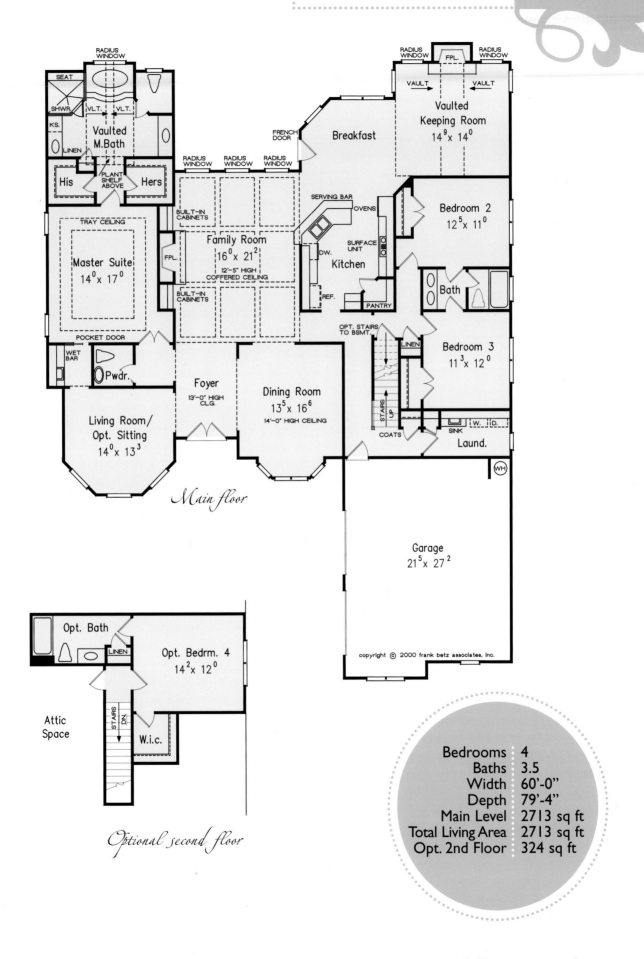

RADIUS WINDOW
SEAT
SHWR.
VLT. VLT.
Vaulted M.Bath
KS.
LINEN
His
PLANT SHELF ABOVE
Hers

RADIUS WINDOW    FPL.    RADIUS WINDOW
VAULT    VAULT
Vaulted Keeping Room
14⁹ x 14⁰

FRENCH DOOR
Breakfast

RADIUS WINDOW    RADIUS WINDOW    RADIUS WINDOW

SERVING BAR    OVENS

Bedroom 2
12⁵ x 11⁰

BUILT-IN CABINETS

TRAY CEILING

Master Suite
14⁰ x 17⁰

FPL.

Family Room
16⁰ x 21²
12'-5" HIGH COFFERED CEILING

DW.
SURFACE UNIT
Kitchen
REF.
PANTRY

Bath

BUILT-IN CABINETS

POCKET DOOR

WET BAR
Pwdr.

Foyer
13'-0" HIGH CLG.

Dining Room
13⁵ x 16⁶
14'-0" HIGH CEILING

OPT. STAIRS TO BSMT.

LINEN

Bedroom 3
11³ x 12⁰

Living Room/ Opt. Sitting
14⁰ x 13³

STAIRS UP

COATS    SINK

W. D.

Laund.

*Main floor*

WH

Garage
21⁵ x 27²

copyright © 2000 frank betz associates, inc.

Opt. Bath
LINEN

Opt. Bedrm. 4
14² x 12⁰

Attic Space

STAIRS DN.

W.i.c.

*Optional second floor*

Bedrooms    4
Baths    3.5
Width    60'-0"
Depth    79'-4"
Main Level    2713 sq ft
Total Living Area    2713 sq ft
Opt. 2nd Floor    324 sq ft

# Allenbrook

Plan Number: MLFB04-3849
Price Code: E

Cheery dormers and a covered front porch give the Allenbrook a friendly, time-tested curb appeal. This design has everything a homeowner needs all on one level. A fireplace lights the cozy keeping room that adjoins the kitchen area. The vaulted family room has an impressive wall of built-in cabinetry and another fireplace. These two living areas give family and guests room to disperse during gatherings. A combination mud and laundry room — with a built-in bench — is located just off the garage. Its split-bedroom design adds an aspect of privacy to the master suite. ■

Foundations Available: Basement or Crawl

*Rear elevation*

The location of casual spaces such as this keeping room makes the space multi-functional. Access to the outdoors and a close relationship to the kitchen and breakfast area help add to the success of such rooms.

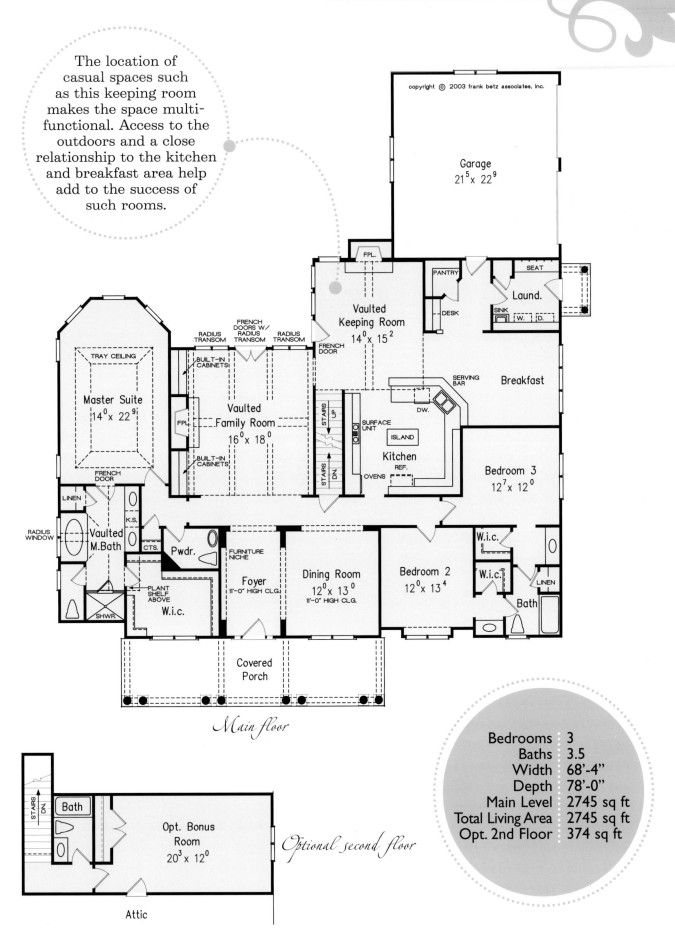

copyright © 2003 frank betz associates, inc.

Garage
21⁵x 22⁹

Vaulted Keeping Room
14⁰x 15²

PANTRY

DESK

SEAT

Laund.

SINK

W. | D.

Master Suite
14⁰x 22⁹

TRAY CEILING

RADIUS TRANSOM

FRENCH DOORS w/ RADIUS TRANSOM

RADIUS TRANSOM

BUILT-IN CABINETS

Vaulted Family Room
16⁰x 18⁰

FRENCH DOOR

STAIRS UP

SERVING BAR

Breakfast

DW.

FPL.

BUILT-IN CABINETS

SURFACE UNIT

ISLAND

Kitchen

REF.

Bedroom 3
12⁷x 12⁰

STAIRS DN

OVENS

FRENCH DOOR

LINEN

RADIUS WINDOW

Vaulted M.Bath

K.S.

CTS.

Pwdr.

FURNITURE NICHE

Foyer
11'-0" HIGH CLG.

Dining Room
12⁰x 13⁰
11'-0" HIGH CLG.

Bedroom 2
12⁰x 13⁴

W.i.c.

W.i.c.

LINEN

Bath

PLANT SHELF ABOVE

SHWR

W.i.c.

*Main floor*

Covered Porch

STAIRS DN

Bath

Opt. Bonus Room
20³x 12⁰

*Optional second floor*

Attic

| | |
|---|---|
| Bedrooms | 3 |
| Baths | 3.5 |
| Width | 68'-4" |
| Depth | 78'-0" |
| Main Level | 2745 sq ft |
| Total Living Area | 2745 sq ft |
| Opt. 2nd Floor | 374 sq ft |

# Stoney River

Plan Number: MLFB04-3866
Price Code: E

Casual elegance and upscale amenities give the Stoney River an edge over its other one-level counterparts. An inviting Old World exterior outside is followed by many unique and special design elements inside. A furniture niche in the foyer creates a place for that special piece that will make an attractive first impression. Coffered ceilings and built-in cabinetry in the family room make this room the natural center-point of the home. A vaulted keeping room adjoins the kitchen area, providing an additional cozy gathering spot. The master suite is accommodating in every sense of the word, with its private sitting room, his-and-her closets, and soaking tub. ◼

Foundations Available: Basement or Crawl

*Rear elevation*

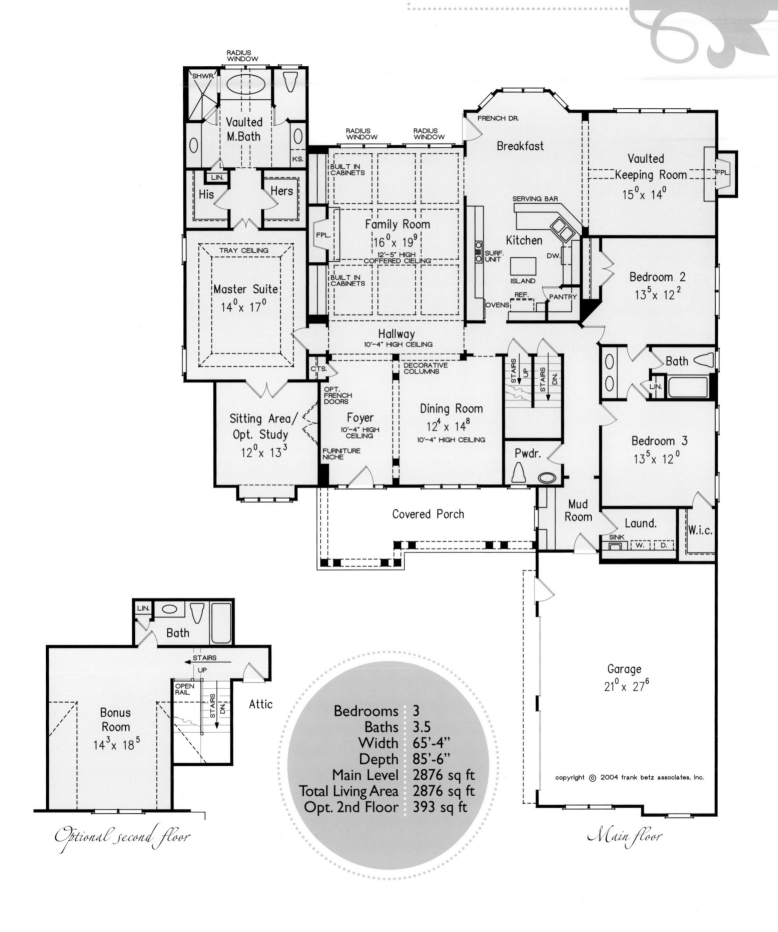

RADIUS WINDOW

SHWR.

Vaulted M.Bath

KS.

LIN.

His    Hers

TRAY CEILING

Master Suite
14⁰ x 17⁰

Sitting Area/
Opt. Study
12⁰ x 13³

CTS.

OPT. FRENCH DOORS

Foyer
10'-4" HIGH CEILING

FURNITURE NICHE

RADIUS WINDOW    RADIUS WINDOW

BUILT IN CABINETS

FPL.

Family Room
16⁰ x 19⁹
12'-5" HIGH COFFERED CEILING

BUILT IN CABINETS

Hallway
10'-4" HIGH CEILING

DECORATIVE COLUMNS

Dining Room
12⁴ x 14⁸
10'-4" HIGH CEILING

FRENCH DR.

Breakfast

SERVING BAR

Kitchen

SURF. UNIT

ISLAND

OVENS    REF.    PANTRY

DW.

Vaulted Keeping Room
15⁰ x 14⁰

FPL

Bedroom 2
13⁵ x 12²

Bath

LIN.

STAIRS UP    STAIRS DN.

Bedroom 3
13⁵ x 12⁰

Pwdr.

Covered Porch

Mud Room

Laund.

SINK    W.    D.

W.i.c.

Garage
21⁰ x 27⁶

copyright © 2004 frank betz associates, inc.

LIN.

Bath

STAIRS UP

OPEN RAIL

STAIRS    STAIRS DN.

Bonus Room
14³ x 18⁵

Attic

*Optional second floor*

| | |
|---|---|
| Bedrooms | 3 |
| Baths | 3.5 |
| Width | 65'-4" |
| Depth | 85'-6" |
| Main Level | 2876 sq ft |
| Total Living Area | 2876 sq ft |
| Opt. 2nd Floor | 393 sq ft |

*Main floor*

# Briarcliff Cottage

Plan Number: MLFB04-3784
Price Code: F

With the common rooms open to each other, the floorplan incorporates a natural traffic flow. The kitchen includes a step-saving design, and for added convenience, the utility room lies adjacent to the kitchen. Decorative ceiling treatments such as the coffered ceiling on the family room and vaulted ceiling in the keeping room, along with flooring options, help differentiate rooms with minimal use of walls. The lower level with a secondary kitchen, fireplace and built-in cabinetry for media equipment is an entertaining family's dream. The garage entrance is conveniently located near the stairway, making the lower level incredibly accessible. ■

Foundations Available: Basement

*Rear elevation*

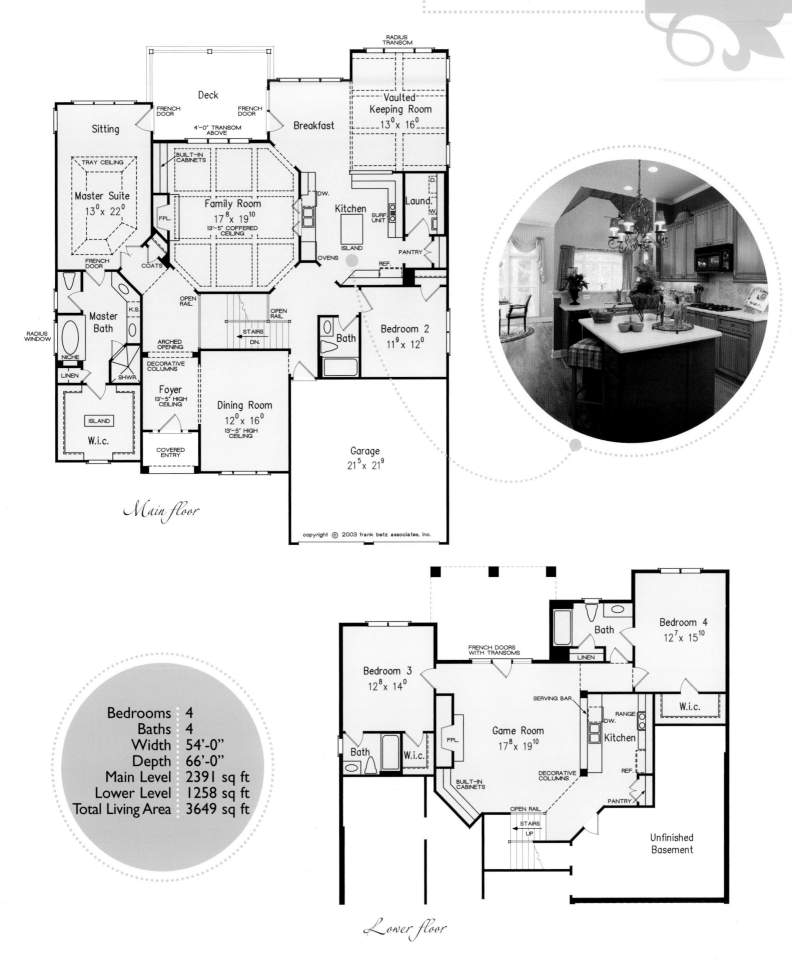

RADIUS
TRANSOM

Deck

Vaulted-
Keeping Room
13⁰ x 16⁰

Sitting

Breakfast

FRENCH
DOOR

FRENCH
DOOR

4'-0" TRANSOM
ABOVE

BUILT-IN
CABINETS

TRAY CEILING

Laund.

Master Suite
13⁰ x 22⁰

DW.

Family Room
17⁸ x 19¹⁰
13'-5" COFFERED
CEILING

Kitchen

SURF
UNIT

FPL.

ISLAND

PANTRY

FRENCH
DOOR

COATS

OVENS

REF.

RADIUS
WINDOW

Master
Bath

K.S.

OPEN
RAIL

OPEN
RAIL

STAIRS
DN.

Bath

Bedroom 2
11⁹ x 12⁰

NICHE

ARCHED
OPENING

LINEN

SHWR.

DECORATIVE
COLUMNS

Foyer
13'-5" HIGH
CEILING

ISLAND

Dining Room
12⁰ x 16⁰
13'-5" HIGH
CEILING

W.i.c.

COVERED
ENTRY

Garage
21⁵ x 21⁹

*Main floor*

copyright © 2003 frank betz associates, inc.

Bedroom 4
12⁷ x 15¹⁰

Bath

FRENCH DOORS
WITH TRANSOMS

LINEN

Bedroom 3
12⁸ x 14⁰

SERVING BAR

RANGE

W.i.c.

FPL.

Game Room
17⁸ x 19¹⁰

DW.

Kitchen

Bath

W.i.c.

REF.

BUILT-IN
CABINETS

DECORATIVE
COLUMNS

PANTRY

OPEN RAIL

STAIRS
UP

Unfinished
Basement

Bedrooms  4
Baths  4
Width  54'-0"
Depth  66'-0"
Main Level  2391 sq ft
Lower Level  1258 sq ft
Total Living Area  3649 sq ft

*Lower floor*

Soaring high-pitched gables reach for the sky. Stone, shake, and board-and-batten siding blend to create a casual façade, so high in demand today.

See more of the Westhampton on page 124.

# MAIN-LEVEL MASTERS

With all the advantages of a one-story home, the home plans in this section combine the ease so many are seeking with the additional space they require. Through smart design, well-proportioned gathering rooms and a pampering master suite enhance daily living on the main-level, while the second floor meets further needs. Filled with trademark characteristics from one of the nation's most accomplished design firms, each home captures a timeless sensibility, even as it looks forward to the future.

Façades showcase numerous styles and a mixture of materials — from the Lowcountry's board-and-batten siding to Old World stone. And each exterior displays keen attention to detail — from cozy Country porches and outdoor living spaces made for alfresco dining to cheery dormers and copper-topped turrets. Interiors are open and versatile, offering livable spaces filled with architectural interest.

For those who want easy living with a bit more space, Main-Level Living was compiled for you, your family and your lifestyle. ■

© 2003 Frank Betz Associates, Inc.

# Aberdeen Place

Plan Number: MLFB04-3809
Price Code: D

*From the Southern Living® Design Collection*, the Aberdeen Place has that cozy cottage appeal with its board-and-batten exterior and stone accents. Its conservative square footage is rich in style and functional design. A warm fireplace anchors the vaulted family room that features access to the deck. The breakfast room is bordered by windows that allow the natural light to pour in. A generously sized master bedroom includes a tray ceiling and views to the backyard. Two bedrooms share a bath on the upper level. An overlook with views to the family room is accessible from both of these rooms. An optional bonus area provides the extra space that each homeowner can personalize. ■

Foundations Available: Basement, Crawl or Slab

*Rear elevation*

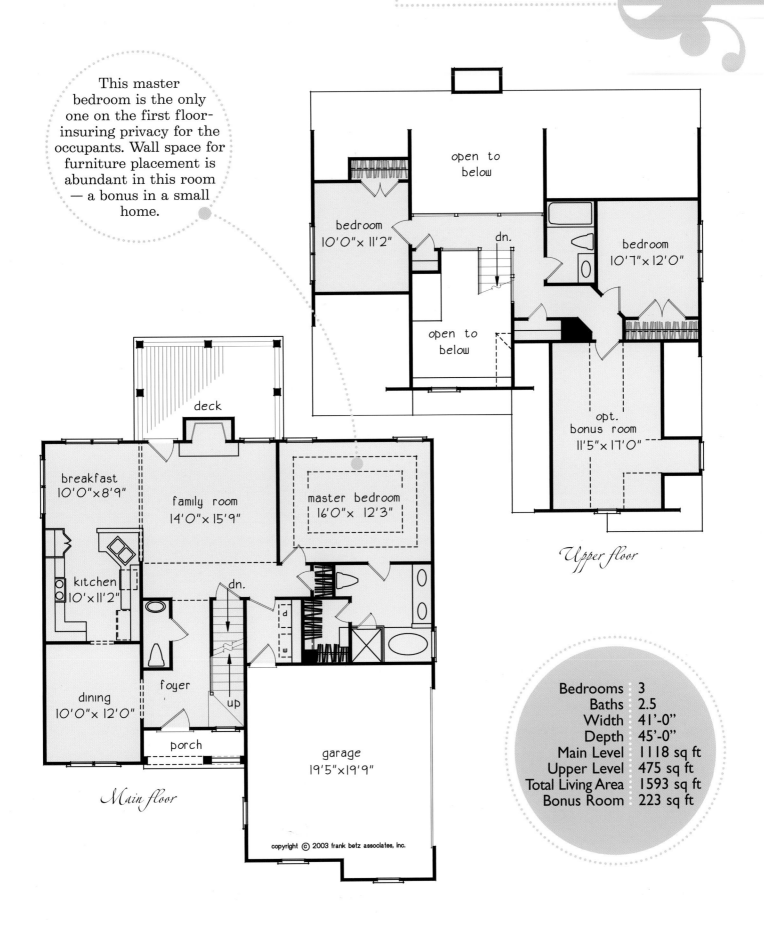

This master bedroom is the only one on the first floor—insuring privacy for the occupants. Wall space for furniture placement is abundant in this room — a bonus in a small home.

open to below

bedroom
10'0" x 11'2"

dn.

bedroom
10'7" x 12'0"

open to below

opt. bonus room
11'5" x 17'0"

*Upper floor*

deck

breakfast
10'0" x 8'9"

family room
14'0" x 15'9"

master bedroom
16'0" x 12'3"

kitchen
10' x 11'2"

dn.

dining
10'0" x 12'0"

foyer

up

porch

garage
19'5" x 19'9"

*Main floor*

copyright © 2003 frank betz associates, inc.

| | |
|---|---|
| Bedrooms | 3 |
| Baths | 2.5 |
| Width | 41'-0" |
| Depth | 45'-0" |
| Main Level | 1118 sq ft |
| Upper Level | 475 sq ft |
| Total Living Area | 1593 sq ft |
| Bonus Room | 223 sq ft |

# Brentwood

Plan Number: MLFB04-3711
Price Code: C

Brick and stone set off by multi-pane windows highlight the street presence of this classic home. A sheltered entry leads to a two-story foyer and wide interior vistas that extend to the back property. Rooms in the public zone are open, allowing the spaces to flex for planned events as well as family gatherings. At the heart of the home, the vaulted family room frames a fireplace with tall windows that bring in natural light. The main-level master suite boasts a tray ceiling, while two upper-level bedrooms are connected by a balcony bridge that overlooks the foyer and family room. ◼

Foundations Available: Basement or Crawl

*Rear elevation*

Family Room
Below

OVERLOOK

Bedroom 3
$10^0$ x $11^5$

Bath

Bedroom 2
$10^7$ x $11^2$

STAIRS DN.

PLANT SHELF

LINEN

Foyer
Below

Opt. Bonus
$11^5$ x $20^6$

*Upper floor*

FPL.

Breakfast

SERVING BAR

TRAY CEILING

Vaulted
Family Room
$14^0$ x $16^6$

Master Suite
$16^0$ x $13^0$

RANGE

Kitchen

DW.

REF.

PANT.

Pwdr.

STAIRS DN.

Laund.

W.i.c.

Vaulted
M.Bath

OPEN RAIL

COATS

Dining Room
$10^0$ x $11^6$

Two Story
Foyer

STAIRS UP

LINEN

SHWR.

STORAGE

COVERED
ENTRY

Garage
$19^5$ x $21^9$

*Main floor*

copyright © 2002 frank betz associates, inc.

| | |
|---|---|
| Bedrooms | 3 |
| Baths | 2.5 |
| Width | 41'-0" |
| Depth | 48'-4" |
| Main Level | 1177 sq ft |
| Upper Level | 457 sq ft |
| Total Living Area | 1634 sq ft |
| Bonus Room | 249 sq ft |

# Foxcrofte

Plan Number: MLFB04-3735
Price Code: C

The Foxcrofte is quaint and charming with its gabled roofline and covered front porch. Vaulted ceilings give a roomy feeling inside in the foyer and great room. The staircase to the upper floor is tucked away near the rear of the home, adding to this design's spaciousness. The dining room is bordered by decorative columns leaving this space open and accessible. Optional bonus space has been incorporated upstairs that presents the opportunity for adding a playroom, home office or craft room. A laundry room and coat closet are placed just inside the garage ensuring coats and shoes stay in their place. ∎

Foundations Available: Basement or Crawl

*Rear elevation*

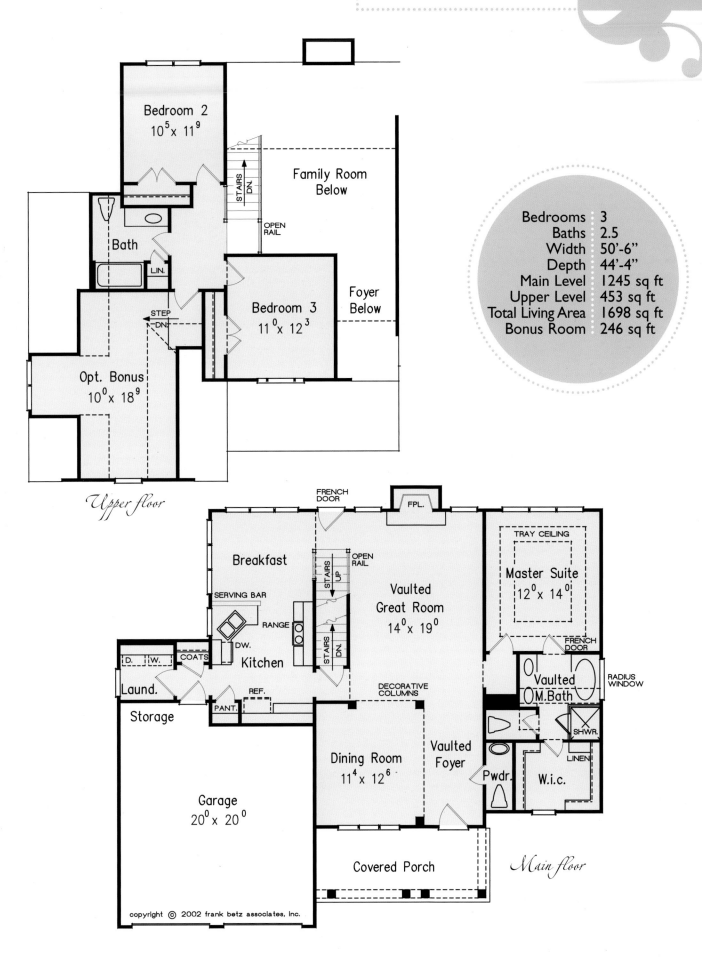

Bedroom 2
$10^5$ x $11^9$

Family Room Below

STAIRS DN.

OPEN RAIL

Bath

LIN.

STEP DN.

Foyer Below

Bedroom 3
$11^0$ x $12^3$

Opt. Bonus
$10^0$ x $18^9$

*Upper floor*

| | |
|---|---|
| Bedrooms | 3 |
| Baths | 2.5 |
| Width | 50'-6" |
| Depth | 44'-4" |
| Main Level | 1245 sq ft |
| Upper Level | 453 sq ft |
| Total Living Area | 1698 sq ft |
| Bonus Room | 246 sq ft |

FRENCH DOOR

FPL.

TRAY CEILING

Breakfast

STAIRS UP

OPEN RAIL

Vaulted Great Room
$14^0$ x $19^0$

Master Suite
$12^0$ x $14^0$

SERVING BAR

RANGE

DW.

Kitchen

STAIRS DN.

FRENCH DOOR

D. W.

COATS

Vaulted M.Bath

RADIUS WINDOW

Laund.

REF.

PANT.

DECORATIVE COLUMNS

SHWR.

Storage

LINEN

Dining Room
$11^4$ x $12^6$

Vaulted Foyer

Pwdr.

W.i.c.

Garage
$20^0$ x $20^0$

Covered Porch

*Main floor*

# Rivermeade

Plan Number: MLFB04-3668
Price Code: D

Volume makes this home feel larger than it is, with vaulted, tray, and two-story ceilings throughout the main level. Day-to-day living is easier because of the attention to details in the design process. A linen closet is situated within the master bedroom closet. The laundry area can also be a mudroom with its direct access off the garage. A handy pass-through from the kitchen to the great room makes entertaining easier. A large covered porch adds interest to the front façade. ■

Foundations Available: Basement or Crawl

*Rear elevation*

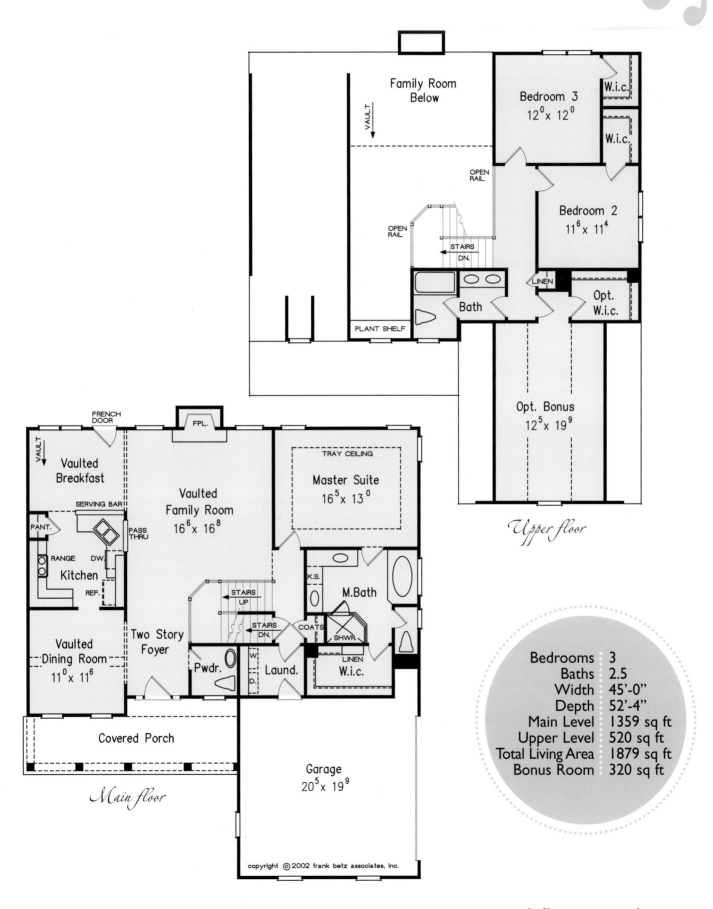

Family Room Below

VAULT

Bedroom 3
12⁰ x 12⁰

W.i.c.

W.i.c.

OPEN RAIL

OPEN RAIL

Bedroom 2
11⁶ x 11⁴

STAIRS DN.

Bath

LINEN

Opt. W.i.c.

PLANT SHELF

Opt. Bonus
12⁵ x 19⁹

*Upper floor*

FRENCH DOOR

FPL.

VAULT

Vaulted Breakfast

TRAY CEILING

Master Suite
16⁵ x 13⁰

SERVING BAR

PASS THRU

Vaulted Family Room
16⁶ x 16⁸

PANT.

RANGE

DW.

Kitchen

REF.

K.S.

M.Bath

STAIRS UP

COATS

SHWR.

LINEN

Vaulted Dining Room
11⁰ x 11⁶

Two Story Foyer

STAIRS DN.

W.i.c.

Pwdr.

W D.

Laund.

Covered Porch

*Main floor*

Garage
20⁵ x 19⁹

| | |
|---|---|
| Bedrooms | 3 |
| Baths | 2.5 |
| Width | 45'-0" |
| Depth | 52'-4" |
| Main Level | 1359 sq ft |
| Upper Level | 520 sq ft |
| Total Living Area | 1879 sq ft |
| Bonus Room | 320 sq ft |

# Stonechase

Plan Number: MLFB04-3662
Price Code: D

Stone accents, carriage doors and board-and-batten shutters come together to create the cottage-like appeal that is so desirable today. The creativity continues inside, where an art niche is positioned as a focal point in the foyer. Continuous arched openings define the dining area. The master suite is secluded from secondary bedrooms, encompassing an entire wing of the main level. A powder room and coat closet are strategically placed near the garage entrance, keeping shoes and coats in their place. The secondary bedrooms have an overlook to the vaulted family room. ■

Foundations Available: Basement or Crawl

*Rear elevation*

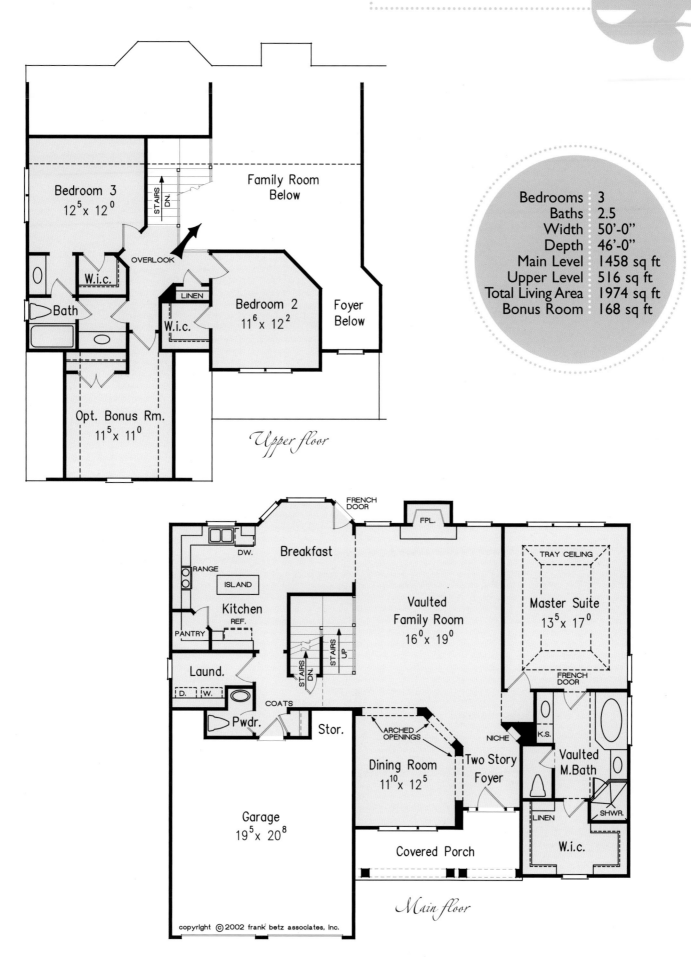

Bedroom 3
$12^5$ x $12^0$

STAIRS DN.

Family Room Below

OVERLOOK

W.i.c.

LINEN

Bath

W.i.c.

Bedroom 2
$11^6$ x $12^2$

Foyer Below

Opt. Bonus Rm.
$11^5$ x $11^0$

*Upper floor*

| | |
|---|---|
| Bedrooms | 3 |
| Baths | 2.5 |
| Width | 50'-0" |
| Depth | 46'-0" |
| Main Level | 1458 sq ft |
| Upper Level | 516 sq ft |
| Total Living Area | 1974 sq ft |
| Bonus Room | 168 sq ft |

FRENCH DOOR

FPL.

DW.

Breakfast

RANGE

ISLAND

TRAY CEILING

Kitchen

REF.

Master Suite
$13^5$ x $17^0$

PANTRY

Vaulted Family Room
$16^0$ x $19^0$

Laund.

STAIRS DN.

STAIRS UP

FRENCH DOOR

D. W.

COATS

Pwdr.

Stor.

ARCHED OPENINGS

NICHE

K.S.

Vaulted M.Bath

Dining Room
$11^{10}$ x $12^5$

Two Story Foyer

LINEN

SHWR.

Garage
$19^5$ x $20^8$

W.i.c.

Covered Porch

*Main floor*

copyright © 2002 frank betz associates, inc.

# Brookhaven

Plan Number: MLFB04-963
Price Code: E

The ageless combination of a covered front porch, brick and classic siding gives the Brookhaven curb appeal that is familiar and friendly. Careful planning inside is evident with highly functional spaces and growth areas. A bedroom on the main level has direct access to a bathing area, making this space an ideal guest room or home office. The upstairs bedrooms feature walk-in closets and share a bath with separate private sink areas. An optional bonus room upstairs leaves homeowners with endless opportunities for finishing this space — a playroom, exercise facility or crafting area are all possibilities. ∎

Foundations Available: Basement, Crawl or Slab

*Rear elevation*

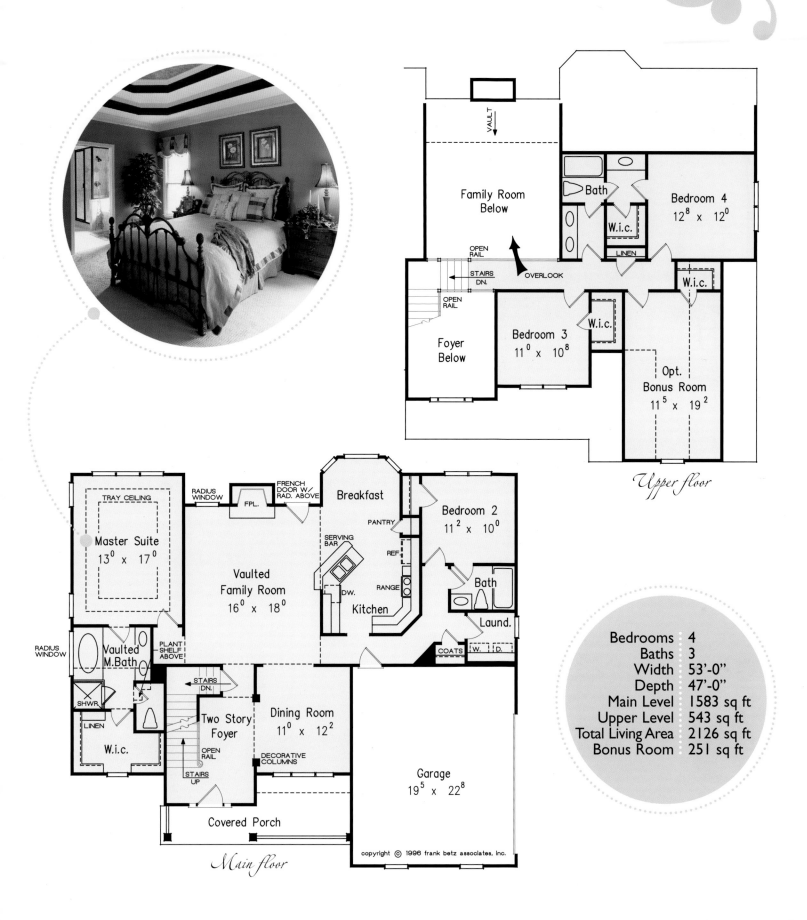

**Family Room Below**

VAULT

Bath

**Bedroom 4**
$12^8$ x $12^0$

W.i.c.

LINEN

OPEN RAIL

STAIRS DN.

OVERLOOK

OPEN RAIL

**Foyer Below**

W.i.c.

**Bedroom 3**
$11^0$ x $10^8$

W.i.c.

**Opt. Bonus Room**
$11^5$ x $19^2$

*Upper floor*

RADIUS WINDOW

FPL.

FRENCH DOOR W/ RAD. ABOVE

**Breakfast**

**Master Suite**
$13^0$ x $17^0$

TRAY CEILING

PANTRY

**Bedroom 2**
$11^2$ x $10^0$

**Vaulted Family Room**
$16^0$ x $18^0$

SERVING BAR

REF.

DW.

RANGE

**Kitchen**

**Bath**

**Laund.**

RADIUS WINDOW

**Vaulted M.Bath**

PLANT SHELF ABOVE

COATS

W.  D.

SHWR.

LINEN

W.i.c.

STAIRS DN.

OPEN RAIL

STAIRS UP

**Two Story Foyer**

**Dining Room**
$11^0$ x $12^2$

DECORATIVE COLUMNS

**Garage**
$19^5$ x $22^8$

**Covered Porch**

*Main floor*

copyright © 1996 frank betz associates, inc.

| | |
|---|---|
| Bedrooms | 4 |
| Baths | 3 |
| Width | 53'-0" |
| Depth | 47'-0" |
| Main Level | 1583 sq ft |
| Upper Level | 543 sq ft |
| Total Living Area | 2126 sq ft |
| Bonus Room | 251 sq ft |

# Colonnade

Plan Number: MLFB04-3699
Price Code: E

Many homeowners today want function with flexibility. The Colonnade was created to provide both of these elements. The family room, kitchen and breakfast area connect to create the home's center point. The size and location of the main-floor bedroom also make it a perfect home office or den. Optional bonus space on the upper level of this home gives homeowners the opportunity to add additional living space to their home. The generous dimensions of this room leave many choices for how the space can be used. One upstairs bedroom has a vaulted ceiling adding unique dimension to the room. ■

Foundations Available: Basement or Crawl

*Rear elevation*

Bedrooms | 4
Baths | 3
Width | 53'-0"
Depth | 47'-6"
Main Level | 1589 sq ft
Upper Level | 549 sq ft
Total Living Area | 2138 sq ft
Bonus Room | 248 sq ft

*Upper floor*

*Main floor*

copyright © 2002 frank betz associates, inc.

# Pasadena

Plan Number: MLFB04-3756
Price Code: E

Charm and character exude from the façade of the
Pasadena with its tapered architectural columns and
carriage doors. Inside, the master suite is tucked away on
the rear of the main level, giving the homeowner a
peaceful place to unwind. An art niche is situated in the
breakfast area, providing the perfect spot for a favorite art
piece or floral arrangement. The kitchen is complete with
a large island, making mealtime easier. Upstairs, an optional
bonus room has been made available that can be used as
the homeowner wishes – a playroom, home office or
fitness room are all fantastic options. ■

Foundations Available: Basement, Crawl or Slab

*Rear elevation*

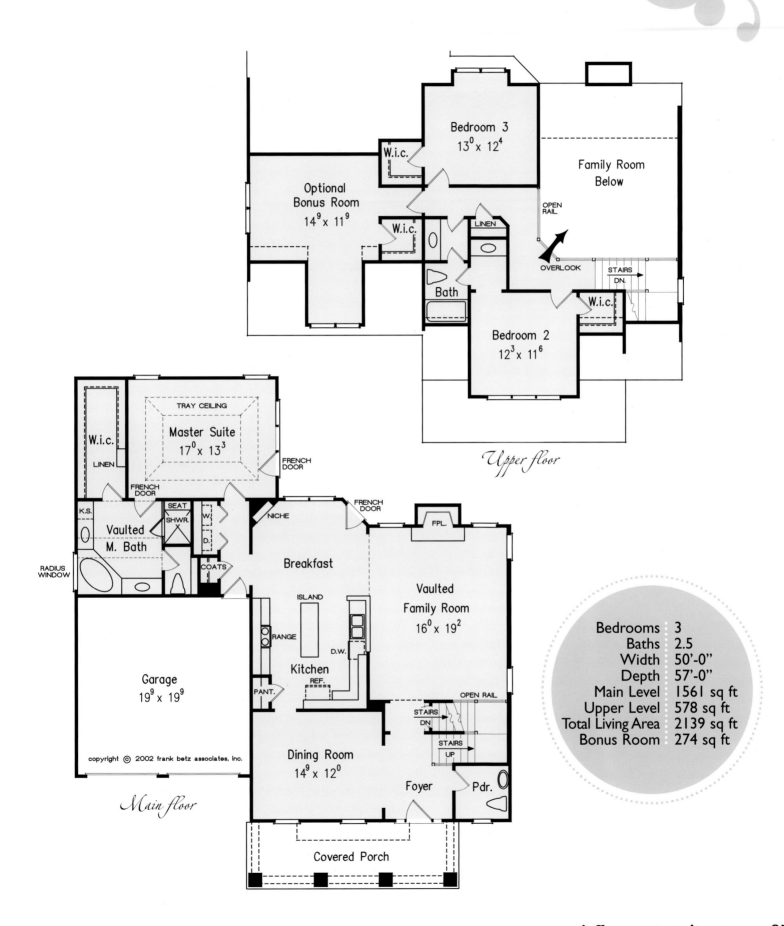

Bedroom 3
13⁰ x 12⁴

Family Room
Below

Optional
Bonus Room
14⁹ x 11⁹

W.i.c.

W.i.c.

LINEN

OPEN RAIL

OVERLOOK

STAIRS DN.

Bath

W.i.c.

Bedroom 2
12³ x 11⁶

*Upper floor*

TRAY CEILING

Master Suite
17⁰ x 13³

W.i.c.

LINEN

FRENCH DOOR

FRENCH DOOR

K.S.

Vaulted
M. Bath

SEAT

SHWR.

W.

D.

COATS

NICHE

FRENCH DOOR

FPL.

RADIUS WINDOW

Breakfast

Vaulted
Family Room
16⁰ x 19²

ISLAND

RANGE

D.W.

Kitchen

REF.

PANT.

OPEN RAIL

Garage
19⁹ x 19⁹

STAIRS DN.

STAIRS UP

copyright © 2002 frank betz associates, inc.

Dining Room
14⁹ x 12⁰

Foyer

Pdr.

*Main floor*

Covered Porch

| | |
|---|---|
| Bedrooms | 3 |
| Baths | 2.5 |
| Width | 50'-0" |
| Depth | 57'-0" |
| Main Level | 1561 sq ft |
| Upper Level | 578 sq ft |
| Total Living Area | 2139 sq ft |
| Bonus Room | 274 sq ft |

# Mallory

Plan Number: MLFB04-992
Price Code: F

Earthy fieldstone and cedar shake accents give the Mallory a casual elegance that Old World style encompasses. Inside, thoughtful consideration was given to this smart and functional floor plan. Everyone knows that family members and guests tend to congregate in the kitchen. The Mallory accommodates this fact, with a vaulted breakfast area and keeping room with fireplace adjoining the kitchen. Two secondary bedrooms — each with a walk-in closet — share a divided bathing area on the second floor. An optional bonus room is ready to finish into a fourth bedroom, playroom or exercise area. ■

Foundations Available: Basement, Crawl or Slab

*Rear elevation*

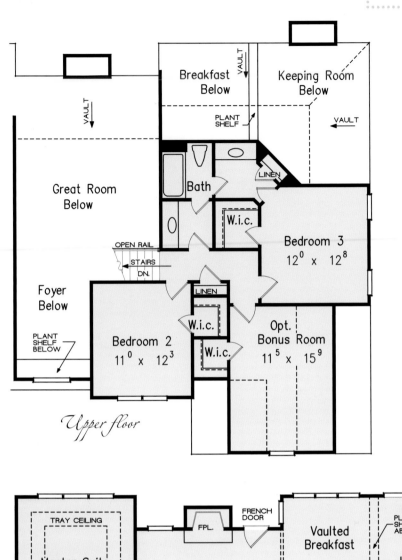

Breakfast Below

Keeping Room Below

VAULT

VAULT

VAULT

PLANT SHELF

Great Room Below

Bath

LINEN

W.i.c.

Bedroom 3
$12^0$ x $12^8$

OPEN RAIL

STAIRS DN.

Foyer Below

LINEN

W.i.c.

PLANT SHELF BELOW

Bedroom 2
$11^0$ x $12^3$

W.i.c.

Opt. Bonus Room
$11^5$ x $15^9$

*Upper floor*

TRAY CEILING

Master Suite
$13^0$ x $17^{3}$

FPL.

FRENCH DOOR

FPL.

Vaulted Breakfast

PLANT SHELF ABOVE

Vaulted Keeping Room
$12^6$ x $15^0$

Vaulted Great Room
$16^0$ x $18^5$

SERVING BAR

DW.

FRENCH DOOR

RADIUS WINDOW

Vaulted M.Bath

COATS

RANGE

Kitchen

PANTRY

Laund.

REF.

W. D.

SHWR.

LINEN

PLANT SHELF ABOVE

Pwdr.

OPEN RAIL

STAIRS DN.

W.i.c.

STAIRS UP

OPEN RAIL

Two Story Foyer

Dining Room
$11^0$ x $12^3$

Garage
$19^5$ x $21^9$

COVERED PORCH

*Main floor*

copyright © 1996 frank betz associates, inc.

| | |
|---|---|
| Bedrooms | 3 |
| Baths | 2.5 |
| Width | 54'-0" |
| Depth | 46'-10" |
| Main Level | 1628 sq ft |
| Upper Level | 527 sq ft |
| Total Living Area | 2155 sq ft |
| Bonus Room | 207 sq ft |

# Azalea Park

Plan Number: MLFB04-3894
Price Code: E

This cozy cottage is as functional inside as it is charming on the outside. The kitchen is equipped with a center island to aid in meal preparation. A mudroom is tucked just off the garage and adjoins the laundry room, keeping coats and shoes in their place. Off the breakfast area, a screened porch makes a great spot for relaxing or outdoor entertaining. Radius windows allow plenty of natural light to illuminate the family room. ■

Foundations Available: Basement or Crawl

*Rear elevation*

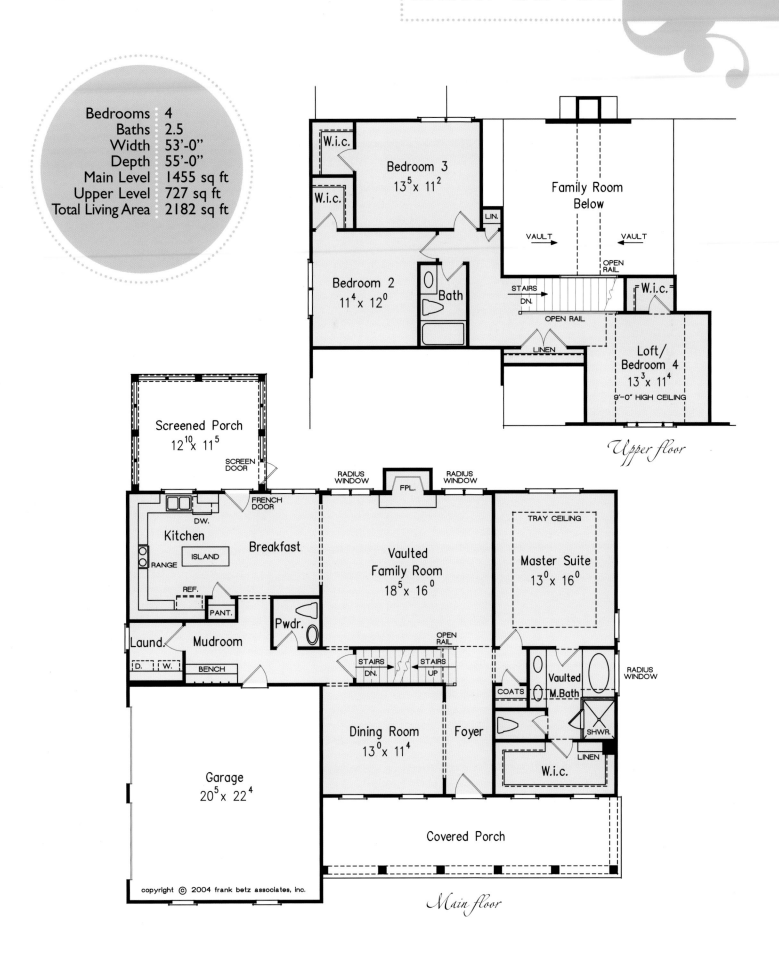

Bedrooms | 4
Baths | 2.5
Width | 53'-0"
Depth | 55'-0"
Main Level | 1455 sq ft
Upper Level | 727 sq ft
Total Living Area | 2182 sq ft

W.i.c.

Bedroom 3
$13^5$ x $11^2$

Family Room Below

VAULT ← → VAULT

W.i.c.

LIN.

OPEN RAIL

Bedroom 2
$11^4$ x $12^0$

Bath

STAIRS DN.

W.i.c.

OPEN RAIL

LINEN

Loft/
Bedroom 4
$13^3$ x $11^4$

9'-0" HIGH CEILING

*Upper floor*

Screened Porch
$12^{10}$ x $11^5$

SCREEN DOOR

RADIUS WINDOW     RADIUS WINDOW

FPL.

FRENCH DOOR

TRAY CEILING

DW.

Kitchen

Breakfast

RANGE

ISLAND

Vaulted
Family Room
$18^5$ x $16^0$

Master Suite
$13^0$ x $16^0$

REF.

PANT.

Pwdr.

Laund.

Mudroom

COATS

OPEN RAIL

Vaulted
M.Bath

RADIUS WINDOW

D.   W.

BENCH

STAIRS DN.   STAIRS UP

SHWR.

LINEN

Garage
$20^5$ x $22^4$

Dining Room
$13^0$ x $11^4$

Foyer

W.i.c.

Covered Porch

copyright © 2004 frank betz associates, inc.

*Main floor*

# Sullivan

Plan Number: MLFB04-1224
Price Code: F

The full brick façade, as well as the classic turret, have stood the test of time. The Sullivan incorporates both of these time-honored design elements. Inside, a well-planned and thoughtful design accommodates the lifestyle of today's homeowner. The home is anchored by a vaulted great room, adjoining the kitchen and breakfast areas allowing easy interaction between family and guests. The master suite is private and well-appointed, complete with his-and-her closets, a lavish bath and comfortable sitting area. An additional main-floor bedroom makes the ideal guest room or can also serve as a home office. An optional bonus room upstairs provides additional space for an exercise area or playroom. ■

Foundations Available: Basement, Crawl or Slab

*Rear elevation*

Bedrooms : 4
Baths : 3
Width : 54'-0"
Depth : 48'-0"
Main Level : 1688 sq ft
Upper Level : 558 sq ft
Total Living Area : 2246 sq ft
Bonus Room : 269 sq ft

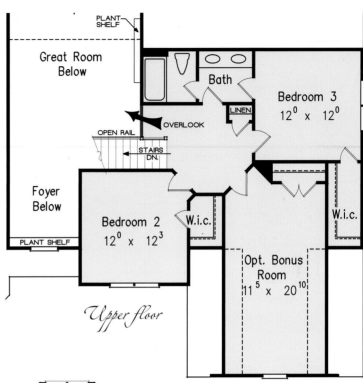

*Upper floor*

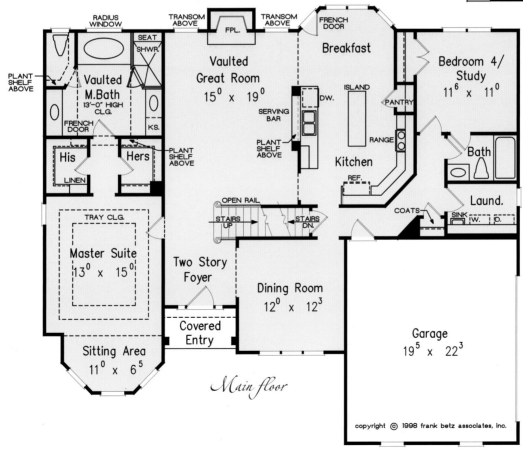

*Main floor*

copyright © 1998 frank betz associates, inc.

# Amelia

Plan Number: MLFB04-3807
Price Code: E

The Amelia's façade is clean and simple, with a cozy front porch and gabled roofline. Board-and-batten shutters and stone accents bring a sense of warmth that is echoed inside this quaint floor plan. A bedroom on the main level is also the perfect location for a home office or den. Upstairs, flexible spaces are incorporated giving the homeowners choices on how to use their space. A loft is situated among the bedrooms making an ideal homework station or lounging area for kids. Optional bonus space is also available, opening up options like a fitness room or media center.

Foundations Available: Basement or Crawl

*Rear elevation*

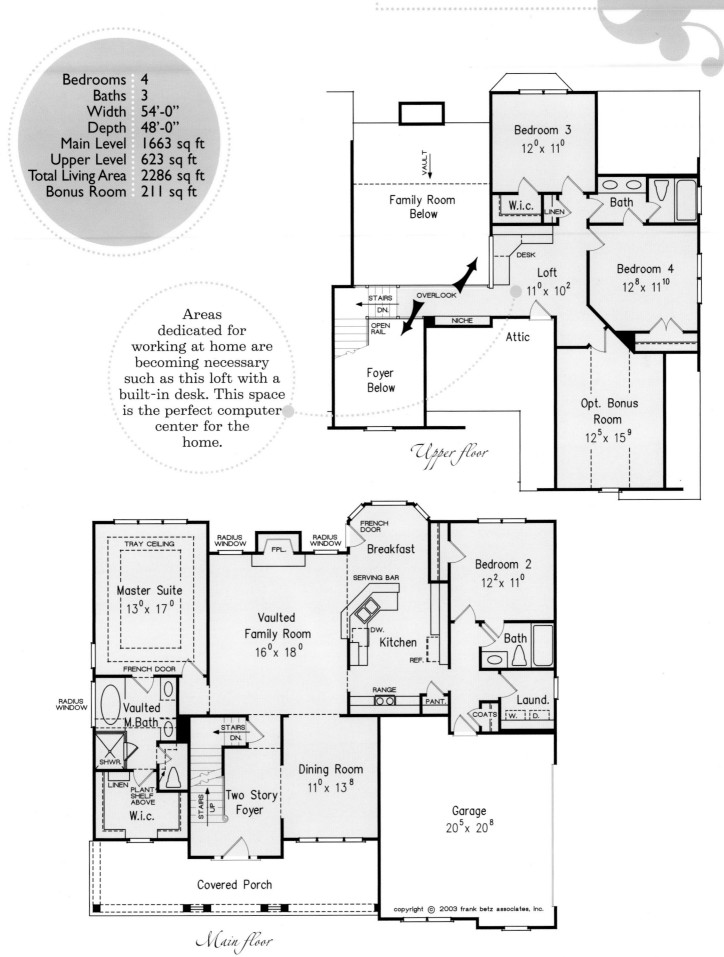

Bedrooms  4
Baths  3
Width  54'-0"
Depth  48'-0"
Main Level  1663 sq ft
Upper Level  623 sq ft
Total Living Area  2286 sq ft
Bonus Room  211 sq ft

Areas dedicated for working at home are becoming necessary such as this loft with a built-in desk. This space is the perfect computer center for the home.

*Upper floor*

*Main floor*

# Macallen

Plan Number: MLFB04-3899
Price Code: D

Beauty is often found in the details! The Macallen has those special touches that personalize a home. A beamed ceiling gives the master suite a rustic and casual elegance that makes it feel like a cottage retreat. A unique vaulted ceiling in the great room affords space for radius transom windows that let the natural light pour into this area. The breakfast room is complete with a built-in desk and access to a screened porch. This space extends the kitchen outside for outdoor entertaining and relaxation. A bench with coat hooks is tucked just off the garage so kids of all ages have a place to unload at the end of the day. ∎

Foundations Available: Basement, Crawl or Slab

*Rear elevation*

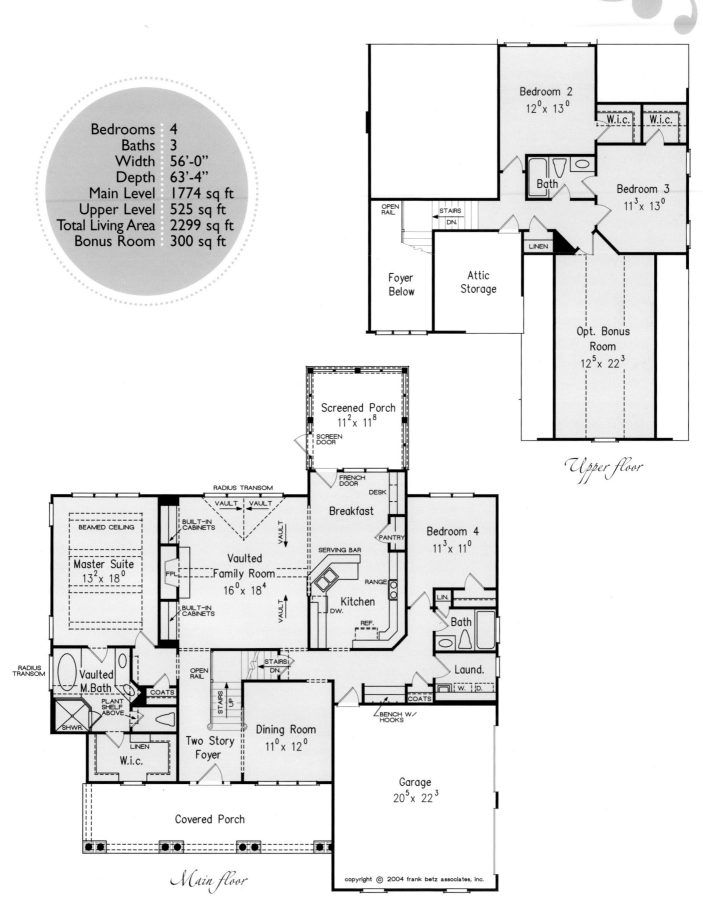

Bedrooms : 4
Baths : 3
Width : 56'-0"
Depth : 63'-4"
Main Level : 1774 sq ft
Upper Level : 525 sq ft
Total Living Area : 2299 sq ft
Bonus Room : 300 sq ft

*Upper floor*

*Main floor*

copyright © 2004 frank betz associates, inc.

# Holly Springs

Plan Number: MLFB04-3821
Price Code: D

The façade of the Holly Springs is eye-catching and original with its unique windows, battered columns, and varied exterior materials. Its Craftsman accents create a casual and welcoming feel from the street. Its main floor houses the master suite, as well as an additional bedroom that makes an ideal guest bedroom with a bath in close proximity. A vaulted breakfast area connects to the kitchen, complete with double ovens and a serving bar. Additional niceties include an arched opening leading to the family room from the foyer and a linen closet in the master suite. ◼

Foundations Available: Basement or Crawl

*Rear elevation*

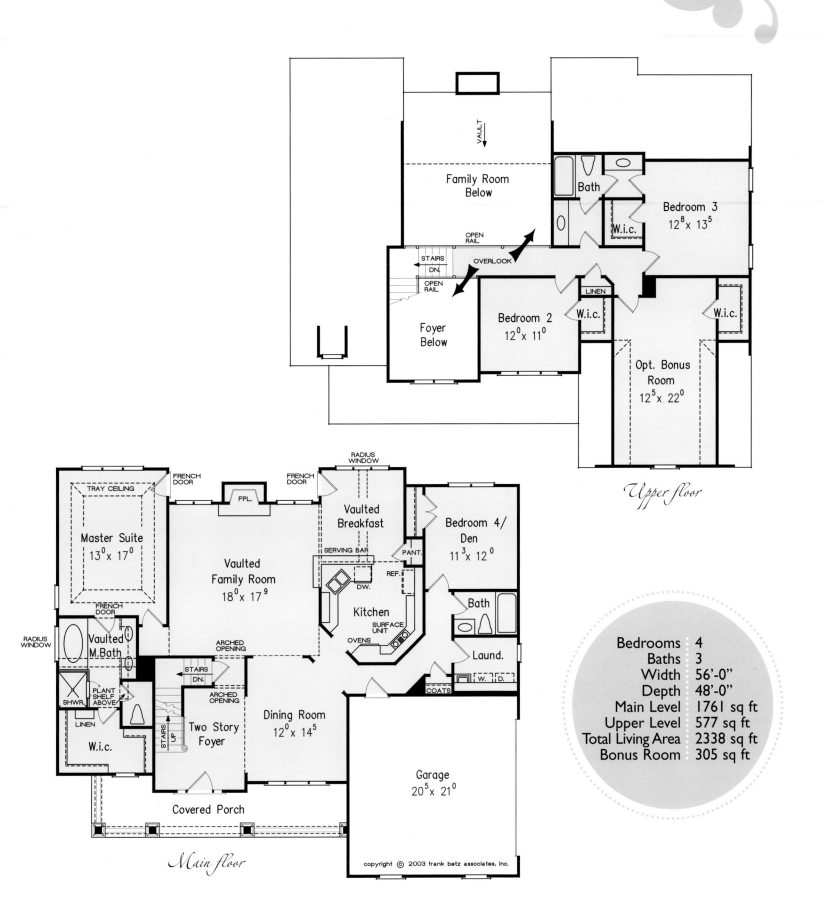

VAULT

Family Room Below

OPEN RAIL

STAIRS DN.

OPEN RAIL

OVERLOOK

Bath

Bedroom 3
$12^8$ x $13^5$

W.i.c.

LINEN

W.i.c.

W.i.c.

Foyer Below

Bedroom 2
$12^0$ x $11^0$

Opt. Bonus Room
$12^5$ x $22^0$

*Upper floor*

TRAY CEILING

FRENCH DOOR

FPL.

FRENCH DOOR

RADIUS WINDOW

FRENCH DOOR

Vaulted Breakfast

Bedroom 4/ Den
$11^3$ x $12^0$

Master Suite
$13^0$ x $17^0$

Vaulted Family Room
$18^0$ x $17^9$

SERVING BAR

PANT.

REF.

RADIUS WINDOW

Vaulted M.Bath

Kitchen

SURFACE UNIT

DW.

Bath

FRENCH DOOR

ARCHED OPENING

OVENS

SURFACE UNIT

PLANT SHELF ABOVE

SHWR.

STAIRS DN.

ARCHED OPENING

Laund.

LINEN

STAIRS UP

Two Story Foyer

Dining Room
$12^0$ x $14^5$

COATS

W. D.

W.i.c.

Garage
$20^5$ x $21^0$

Covered Porch

*Main floor*

copyright © 2003 frank betz associates, inc.

| | |
|---|---|
| Bedrooms | 4 |
| Baths | 3 |
| Width | 56'-0" |
| Depth | 48'-0" |
| Main Level | 1761 sq ft |
| Upper Level | 577 sq ft |
| Total Living Area | 2338 sq ft |
| Bonus Room | 305 sq ft |

# Hanley Hall

Plan Number: MLFB04-1256
Price Code: F

*From the Southern Living® Design Collection -* The main floor has everything a family would want in a home. A spacious family room – with a two-story ceiling – is the focal point for activity. It opens to the dining and breakfast rooms. The kitchen also functions as a center for activity — its openness allows the cook to interact with anyone in adjoining rooms. One bedroom with a full bath is located in its own corner of the plan. Privacy and convenient access to the garage make this room ideal for guests or an additional family member staying for an extended visit. The master bedroom is on the other side of the house. On the second floor, two additional bedrooms share a full bath. The bonus space is ideal for a playroom, media room or home office. ■

Foundations Available: Basement, Crawl or Slab

*Rear elevation*

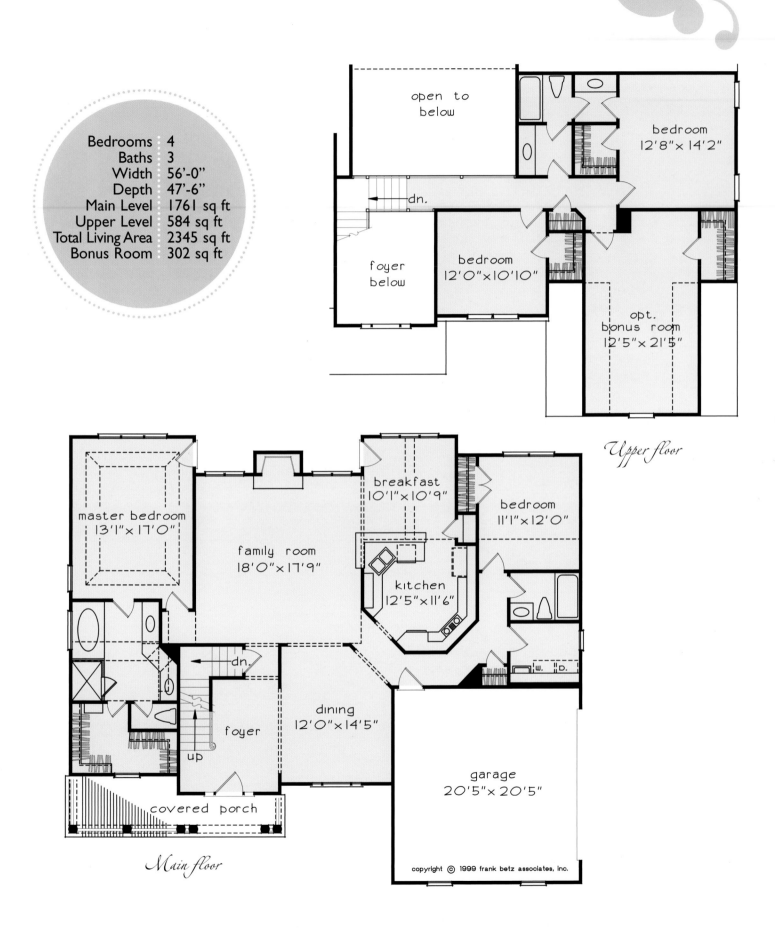

Bedrooms | 4
Baths | 3
Width | 56'-0"
Depth | 47'-6"
Main Level | 1761 sq ft
Upper Level | 584 sq ft
Total Living Area | 2345 sq ft
Bonus Room | 302 sq ft

open to below

bedroom
12'8" × 14'2"

dn.

foyer below

bedroom
12'0" × 10'10"

opt. bonus room
12'5" × 21'5"

*Upper floor*

master bedroom
13'1" × 17'0"

family room
18'0" × 17'9"

breakfast
10'1" × 10'9"

bedroom
11'1" × 12'0"

kitchen
12'5" × 11'6"

w. D.

dn.

foyer

up

dining
12'0" × 14'5"

garage
20'5" × 20'5"

covered porch

*Main floor*

copyright © 1999 frank betz associates, inc.

# Catawba Ridge

Plan Number: MLFB04-3823
Price Code: E

*From the Southern Living® Design Collection* - Charm and character exude from the inviting exterior of Catawba Ridge with its welcoming combination of stone and cedar shake. A cozy front porch graces the front of the home. Inside, the kitchen, breakfast area and family room are conveniently grouped together for easy family interaction. Just off the breakfast area is a comfy screened porch – the perfect spot to end a busy day. The master suite encompasses an entire wing of the home, giving the homeowner added privacy. Kids will love having their own designated spot to do homework in the computer loft upstairs. An optional bonus room is ready to finish on the upper level, ideal for a fourth bedroom, play area or exercise room. ■

Foundations Available: Basement, Crawl or Slab

*Rear elevation*

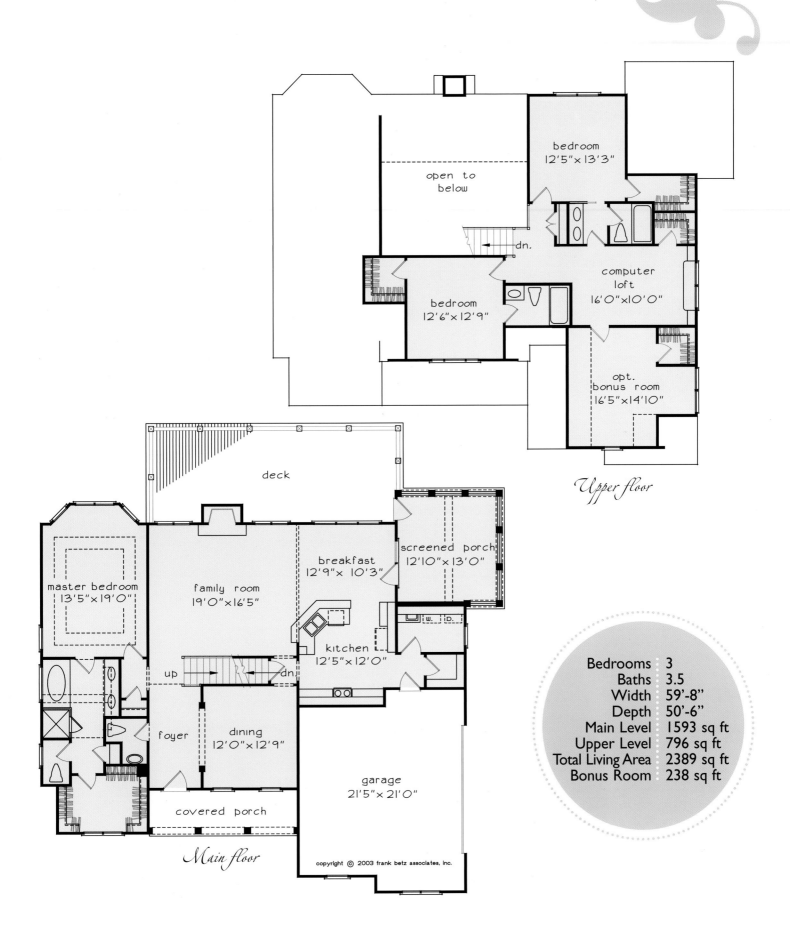

bedroom
12'5"x 13'3"

open to
below

dn.

computer
loft
16'0"x10'0"

bedroom
12'6"x 12'9"

opt.
bonus room
16'5"x14'10"

*Upper floor*

deck

screened porch
12'10"x 13'0"

breakfast
12'9"x 10'3"

master bedroom
13'5"x 19'0"

family room
19'0"x16'5"

kitchen
12'5"x 12'0"

w. D.

up

dn

foyer

dining
12'0"x 12'9"

garage
21'5"x 21'0"

covered porch

*Main floor*

copyright © 2003 frank betz associates, inc.

| | |
|---|---|
| Bedrooms | 3 |
| Baths | 3.5 |
| Width | 59'-8" |
| Depth | 50'-6" |
| Main Level | 1593 sq ft |
| Upper Level | 796 sq ft |
| Total Living Area | 2389 sq ft |
| Bonus Room | 238 sq ft |

# Tullamore Square

Plan Number: MLFB04-3801
Price Code: E

This home is every bit as quaint as its name with a cedar shake exterior accented with a rooftop cupola. Its interior is simple, functional and full of pleasant surprises that make everyday living a little easier. Its master suite encompasses an entire side of the lower level, with a large sitting area perfectly suited for a comfy lounge chair. A seated shower, soaking tub and his-and-her closets make the master bath feel like five-star luxury. A coat closet and a laundry room are placed just off the garage, keeping coats and shoes in their place. A second main-floor bedroom makes a great guest room or home office. ■

Foundations Available: Basement or Crawl

*Rear elevation*

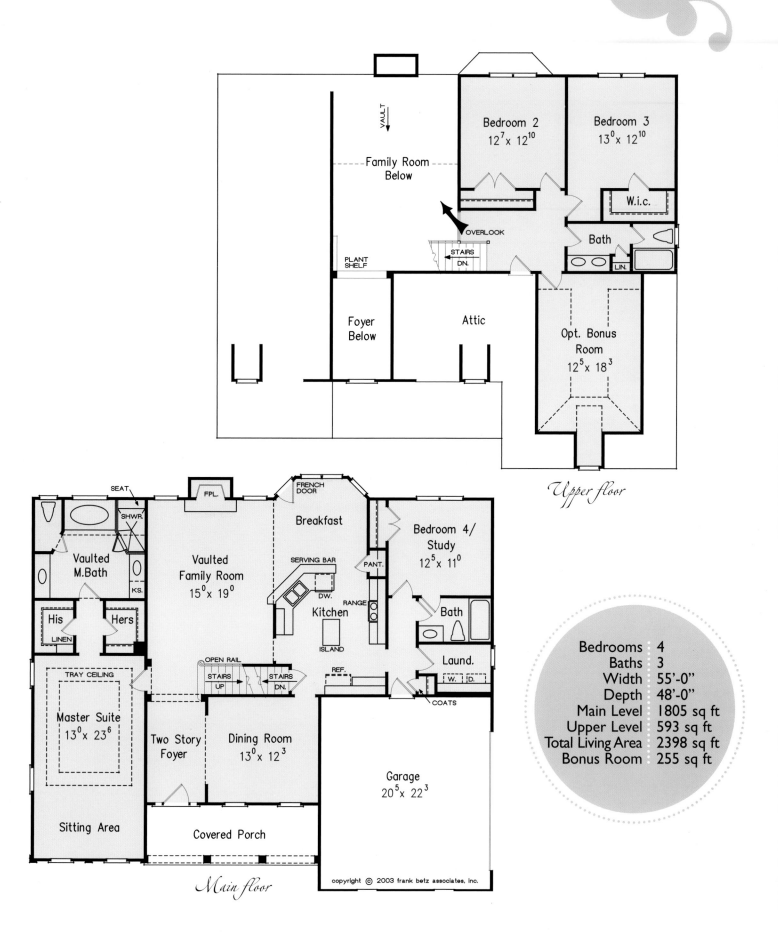

VAULT

Bedroom 2
12⁷ x 12¹⁰

Bedroom 3
13⁰ x 12¹⁰

Family Room
Below

W.i.c.

OVERLOOK

Bath

STAIRS
DN.

LIN.

PLANT
SHELF

Foyer
Below

Attic

Opt. Bonus
Room
12⁵ x 18³

*Upper floor*

SEAT

FPL.

FRENCH
DOOR

SHWR.

Breakfast

Bedroom 4/
Study
12⁵ x 11⁰

Vaulted
M.Bath

Vaulted
Family Room
15⁰ x 19⁰

SERVING BAR

KS.

DW.

PANT.

HIS

HERS

RANGE

Bath

LINEN

Kitchen

ISLAND

Laund.

TRAY CEILING

OPEN RAIL

REF.

W. D.

STAIRS
UP

STAIRS
DN.

COATS

Master Suite
13⁰ x 23⁶

Two Story
Foyer

Dining Room
13⁰ x 12³

Garage
20⁵ x 22³

Sitting Area

Covered Porch

*Main floor*

| | |
|---|---|
| Bedrooms | 4 |
| Baths | 3 |
| Width | 55'-0" |
| Depth | 48'-0" |
| Main Level | 1805 sq ft |
| Upper Level | 593 sq ft |
| Total Living Area | 2398 sq ft |
| Bonus Room | 255 sq ft |

# Addison Place

Plan Number: MLFB04-3781
Price Code: D

A courtyard entry and dormered roofline create interesting dimension on the façade of the Addison Place. Subtle separation between the kitchen and keeping room allows for privacy, but still provides easy access from one to the other. Built-in cabinets allow homeowners to decorate with their own personal touch. Both bedrooms upstairs feature the luxury of a walk-in closet and share a divided bath. A large bonus area is available on the upper level that can be finished to suit the needs of the homeowner as a guest suite, media room or fourth bedroom. ■

Foundations Available: Basement or Crawl

*Rear elevation*

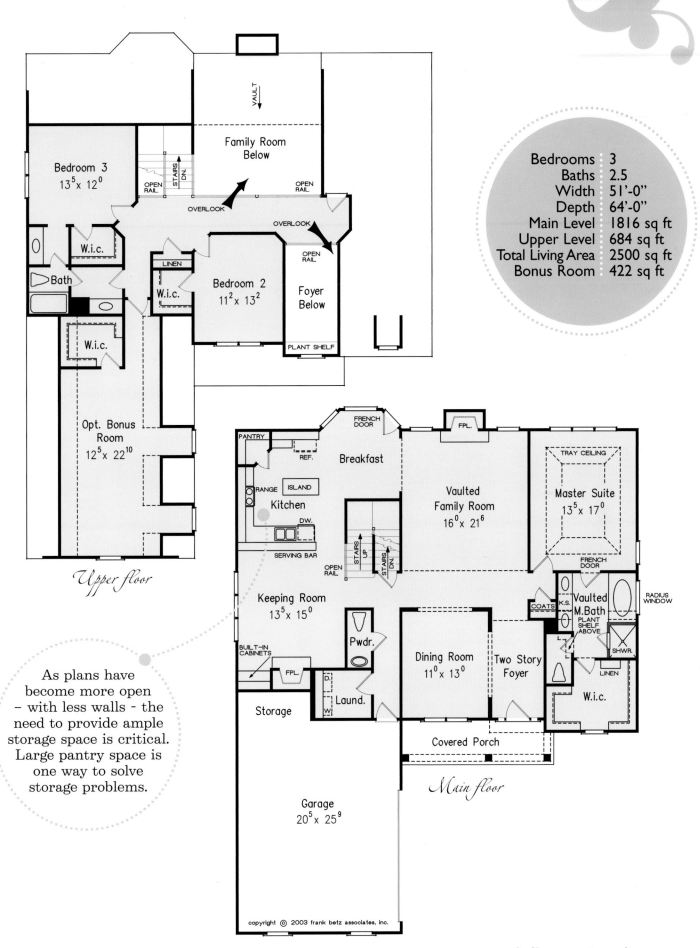

**Upper floor**

**Main floor**

Bedrooms 3
Baths 2.5
Width 51'-0"
Depth 64'-0"
Main Level 1816 sq ft
Upper Level 684 sq ft
Total Living Area 2500 sq ft
Bonus Room 422 sq ft

As plans have become more open – with less walls - the need to provide ample storage space is critical. Large pantry space is one way to solve storage problems.

copyright © 2003 frank betz associates, inc.

# Bainbridge Court

Plan Number: MLFB04-3815
Price Code: E

*From the Southern Living® Design Collection* - The classic brick-and-siding exterior of the Bainbridge Court gives this home a time-honored elegant appeal. The staircase is strategically tucked away to keep the foyer open and roomy. A cozy screened porch adjoins the kitchen area and has access to an expansive deck, making a great space for grilling and entertaining. Two bedrooms — the master suite and a guest room — share the main level of the home. This guest room converts easily into a home office for the telecommuter, at-home mom or retiree. On the upper level, three well-placed bedrooms share a bath and enjoy overlook views into the family room. ■

Foundations Available: Basement, Crawl or Slab

*Rear elevation*

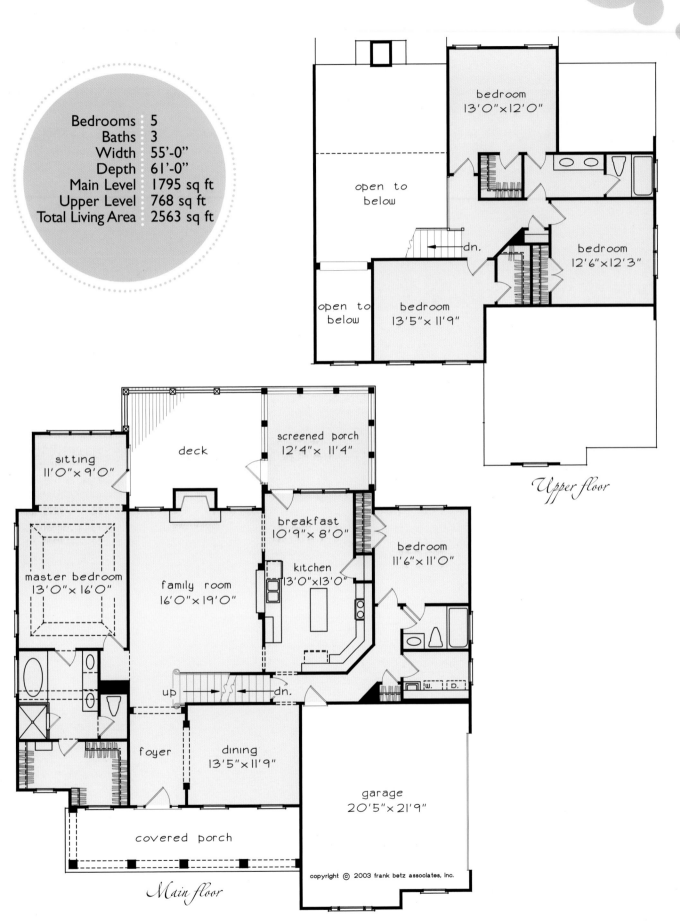

Bedrooms 5
Baths 3
Width 55'-0"
Depth 61'-0"
Main Level 1795 sq ft
Upper Level 768 sq ft
Total Living Area 2563 sq ft

bedroom
13'0"x12'0"

open to below

dn.

bedroom
12'6"x12'3"

open to below

bedroom
13'5"x11'9"

*Upper floor*

deck

sitting
11'0"x9'0"

screened porch
12'4"x 11'4"

breakfast
10'9"x 8'0"

master bedroom
13'0"x16'0"

family room
16'0"x19'0"

kitchen
13'0"x13'0"

bedroom
11'6"x11'0"

up

dn.

W. D.

foyer

dining
13'5"x11'9"

garage
20'5"x21'9"

covered porch

copyright © 2003 frank betz associates, inc.

*Main floor*

# Greythorne

Plan Number: MLFB04-3764
Price Code: F

Vertical siding lends a rural influence to this stately brick façade, with rustic shutters and copper-seam roofs that further the sense of informality. An open arrangement of the foyer, dining room and vaulted grand room define the public realm, designed to take advantage of the views and natural light brought in by tall rear windows. Coffered ceilings add texture to the kitchen and breakfast area, which is open to a vaulted keeping room. Arched transoms and access to the rear covered porch enliven this casual space and help to create an inviting retreat for the family. A vaulted bath, a window seat and private access to the porch enhance the master suite. ■

Foundations Available: Basement or Crawl

*Rear elevation*

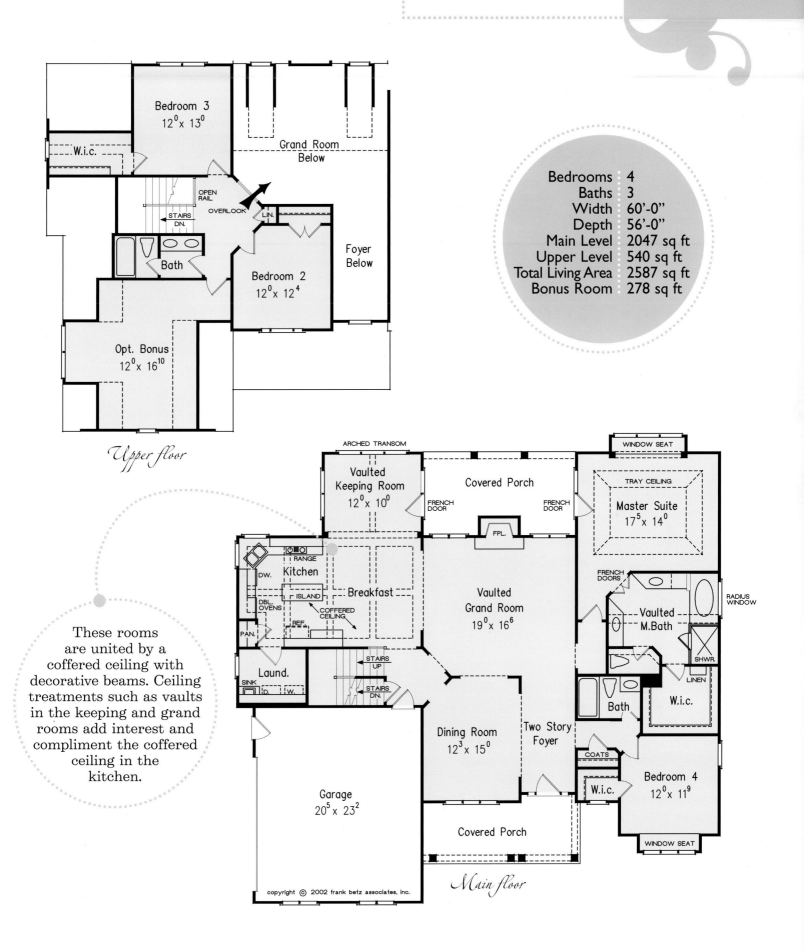

**Bedroom 3**
12⁰ x 13⁰

W.i.c.

Grand Room
Below

OPEN RAIL

OVERLOOK

LIN.

STAIRS DN.

**Bath**

**Bedroom 2**
12⁰ x 12⁴

Foyer Below

**Opt. Bonus**
12⁰ x 16¹⁰

*Upper floor*

| Bedrooms | 4 |
|---|---|
| Baths | 3 |
| Width | 60'-0" |
| Depth | 56'-0" |
| Main Level | 2047 sq ft |
| Upper Level | 540 sq ft |
| Total Living Area | 2587 sq ft |
| Bonus Room | 278 sq ft |

ARCHED TRANSOM

**Vaulted Keeping Room**
12⁰ x 10⁰

FRENCH DOOR

Covered Porch

FRENCH DOOR

WINDOW SEAT

TRAY CEILING

**Master Suite**
17⁵ x 14⁰

RANGE

DW.

**Kitchen**

ISLAND

DBL. OVENS

COFFERED CEILING

REF.

PAN.

**Breakfast**

FPL.

**Vaulted Grand Room**
19⁰ x 16⁶

FRENCH DOORS

**Vaulted M.Bath**

RADIUS WINDOW

SHWR.

LINEN

These rooms are united by a coffered ceiling with decorative beams. Ceiling treatments such as vaults in the keeping and grand rooms add interest and compliment the coffered ceiling in the kitchen.

**Laund.**

SINK

D. W.

STAIRS UP

STAIRS DN.

**Bath**

**W.i.c.**

**Dining Room**
12³ x 15⁰

Two Story Foyer

COATS

W.i.c.

**Bedroom 4**
12⁰ x 11⁹

**Garage**
20⁵ x 23²

Covered Porch

WINDOW SEAT

copyright © 2002 frank betz associates, inc.

*Main floor*

# Rosemore Place

Plan Number: MLFB04-3787
Price Code: E

Distinctive fieldstone and cedar shake give the façade of the Rosemore Place warm texture and dimension. This warmth radiates inside as well with a fire-lit keeping room just off the kitchen. The master suite is private and secluded on the main level of the home. A private sitting area personalizes this space. The main-floor bedroom can act as the home office — perfect for the telecommuter or entrepreneur. An optional bonus room is designed for the upper floor with endless possibilities – a fifth bedroom, recreation room, or fitness area would all be easily accommodated by this space.  ■

Foundations Available: Basement or Crawl

*Rear elevation*

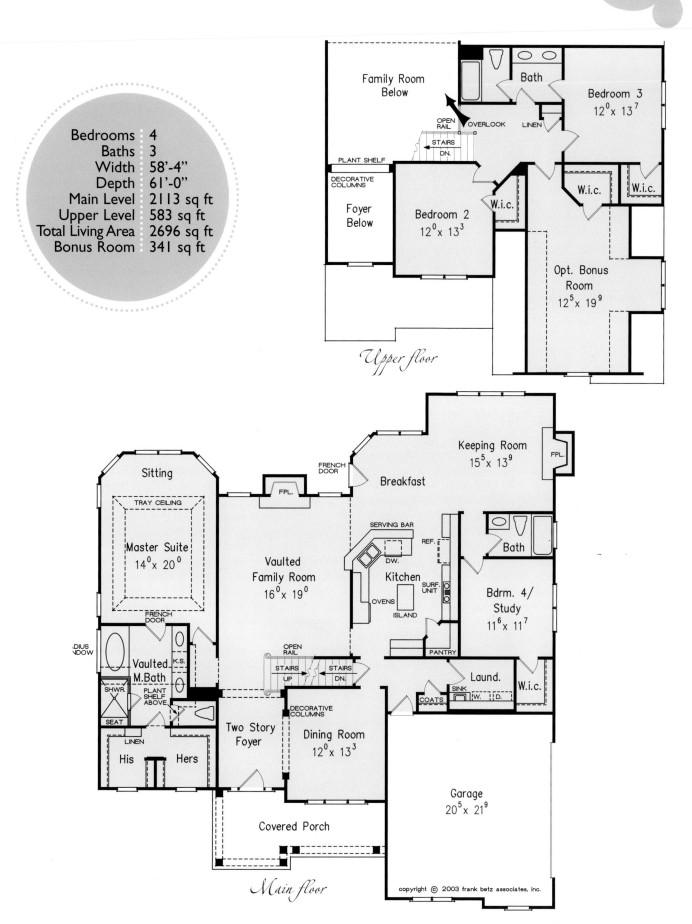

Bedrooms | 4
Baths | 3
Width | 58'-4"
Depth | 61'-0"
Main Level | 2113 sq ft
Upper Level | 583 sq ft
Total Living Area | 2696 sq ft
Bonus Room | 341 sq ft

Family Room Below

Bath

Bedroom 3
$12^0$ x $13^7$

OPEN RAIL

OVERLOOK

LINEN

STAIRS DN.

PLANT SHELF

DECORATIVE COLUMNS

Foyer Below

Bedroom 2
$12^0$ x $13^3$

W.i.c.

W.i.c.

W.i.c.

Opt. Bonus Room
$12^5$ x $19^9$

*Upper floor*

Sitting

TRAY CEILING

Master Suite
$14^0$ x $20^0$

FRENCH DOOR

Keeping Room
$15^5$ x $13^9$

FPL.

FPL.

FRENCH DOOR

Breakfast

SERVING BAR

REF.

Bath

Vaulted Family Room
$16^0$ x $19^0$

DW.

Kitchen

SURF. UNIT

Bdrm. 4/ Study
$11^6$ x $11^7$

.DIUS NDOW

Vaulted M.Bath

K.S.

OVENS

ISLAND

PANTRY

SHWR.

PLANT SHELF ABOVE

OPEN RAIL

STAIRS UP

STAIRS DN.

Laund.

SINK

W.i.c.

SEAT

COATS

W.   D.

LINEN

His

Hers

Two Story Foyer

DECORATIVE COLUMNS

Dining Room
$12^0$ x $13^3$

Garage
$20^5$ x $21^9$

Covered Porch

*Main floor*

copyright © 2003 frank betz associates, inc.

# North Easton

Plan Number: MLFB04-3901
Price Code: E

The North Easton is packed with pleasant surprises in every direction. A coffered ceiling in the family room makes a dramatic focal point for the design. Raised bar seating on the kitchen island provides a casual dining spot or additional seating for entertaining. A mudroom just off the garage has a bench with coat hooks incorporated into it, giving book bags and kids' coats a designated drop spot. The master suite is the only bedroom on the main floor, giving homeowners the privacy they desire. Upstairs, a children's recreation room provides the ideal spot for playing and lounging.

Foundations Available: Crawl or Slab

*Rear elevation*

**Recreation Room**
$16^0$ x $18^3$

Attic

**Bedroom 3**
$13^8$ x $11^6$

STAIRS UP

W.i.c.

OPEN RAIL

STAIRS UP

STAIRS DN

W.i.c.

W.i.c.

Bath

LINEN

**Bedroom 2**
$13^8$ x $12^5$

*Upper floor*

STAIRS DN

OPEN RAIL

**Bonus Room**
$21^6$ x $19^5$

*Optional third floor*

A large space such as this recreation room allows many options to the homeowner. Media, games and lounging are all popular choices for such spaces.

Bedrooms 3
Baths 2.5
Width 46'-0"
Depth 85'-0"
Main Level 1725 sq ft
Upper Level 992 sq ft
Total Living Area 2717 sq ft
Opt. 3rd Floor 351 sq ft

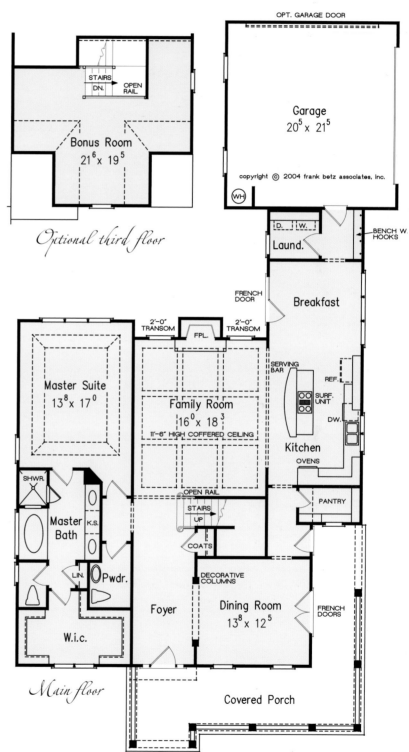

OPT. GARAGE DOOR

**Garage**
$20^5$ x $21^5$

copyright © 2004 frank betz associates, inc.

WH

D. W.

Laund.

BENCH W. HOOKS

Breakfast

FRENCH DOOR

SERVING BAR

REF.

2'-0" TRANSOM

FPL.

2'-0" TRANSOM

SURF. UNIT

DW.

**Master Suite**
$13^8$ x $17^0$

**Family Room**
$16^0$ x $18^3$
11'-6" HIGH COFFERED CEILING

Kitchen

OVENS

PANTRY

SHWR.

K.S.

OPEN RAIL

STAIRS UP

**Master Bath**

LIN.

Pwdr.

COATS

DECORATIVE COLUMNS

W.i.c.

Foyer

**Dining Room**
$13^8$ x $12^5$

FRENCH DOORS

*Main floor*

Covered Porch

# Keeneland

Plan Number: MLFB04-3758
Price Code: E

Craftsman-style detailing gives the façade of the Keeneland the extra zest that many homeowners are in search of. Fieldstone and timber accents create a sense of warmth and welcome. Distinctive design elements can be found throughout this home. A cozy keeping room with a fireplace adjoins the kitchen and breakfast areas, creating a comfortable place to relax or entertain. Upstairs, a family center has been cleverly incorporated, wisely utilizing all of the available space on this floor. Many opt to use it as a multi-purpose family room, housing the computer, a television, toys or exercise equipment. ▪

Foundations Available: Basement or Crawl

*Rear elevation*

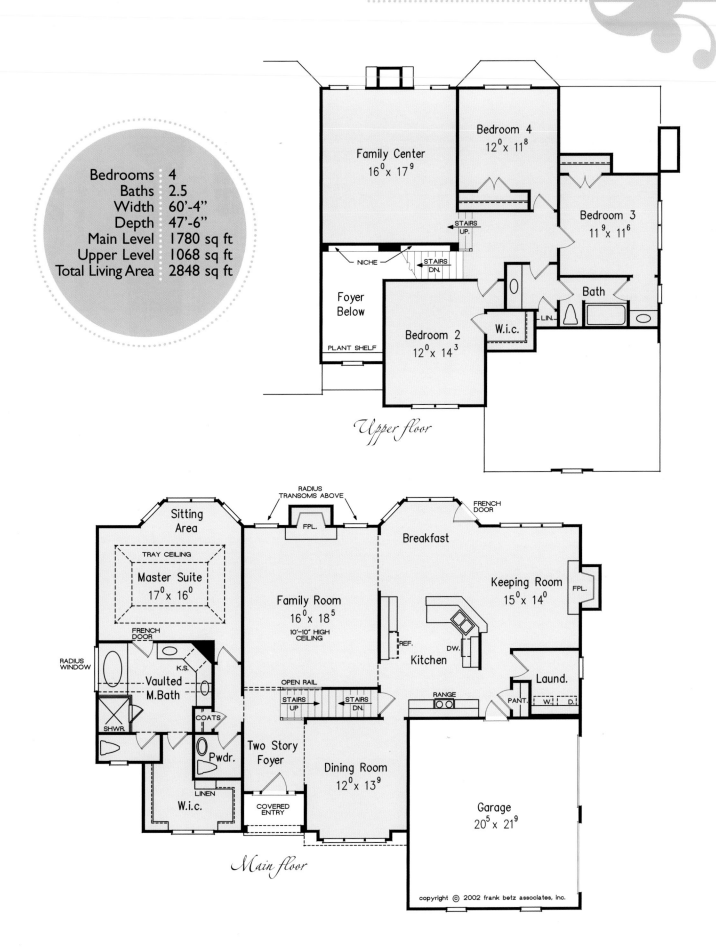

Bedrooms | 4
Baths | 2.5
Width | 60'-4"
Depth | 47'-6"
Main Level | 1780 sq ft
Upper Level | 1068 sq ft
Total Living Area | 2848 sq ft

Family Center
$16^0$ x $17^9$

Bedroom 4
$12^0$ x $11^8$

Bedroom 3
$11^9$ x $11^6$

STAIRS UP.

NICHE

STAIRS DN.

Foyer Below

Bath

W.i.c.

LIN.

Bedroom 2
$12^0$ x $14^3$

PLANT SHELF

*Upper floor*

RADIUS TRANSOMS ABOVE

FRENCH DOOR

Sitting Area

FPL.

Breakfast

TRAY CEILING

Master Suite
$17^0$ x $16^0$

Keeping Room
$15^0$ x $14^0$

FPL.

Family Room
$16^0$ x $18^5$
10'-10" HIGH CEILING

FRENCH DOOR

RADIUS WINDOW

K.S.

Vaulted M.Bath

REF.

Kitchen

DW.

Laund.

COATS

SHWR.

OPEN RAIL

STAIRS UP

STAIRS DN.

RANGE

PANT.

W. D.

Pwdr.

Two Story Foyer

Dining Room
$12^0$ x $13^9$

LINEN

W.i.c.

COVERED ENTRY

Garage
$20^5$ x $21^9$

*Main floor*

copyright © 2002 frank betz associates, inc.

# Braddock

Plan Number: MLFB04-3725
Price Code: F

Brick and siding give the Braddock a traditional flair on the outside, while today's most popular features are incorporated inside. A vaulted keeping room acts as a cozy extension of the kitchen and breakfast areas. The master suite is private and secluded, being the only bedroom on the main level of the home. French doors lead to a lush master bath, equipped with all the creature comforts – dual sinks, linen closet and a soaking tub. Flexible space is incorporated into this design with a fifth bedroom that can remain as such, or easily convert into a study. ■

Foundations Available: Basement or Crawl

*Rear elevation*

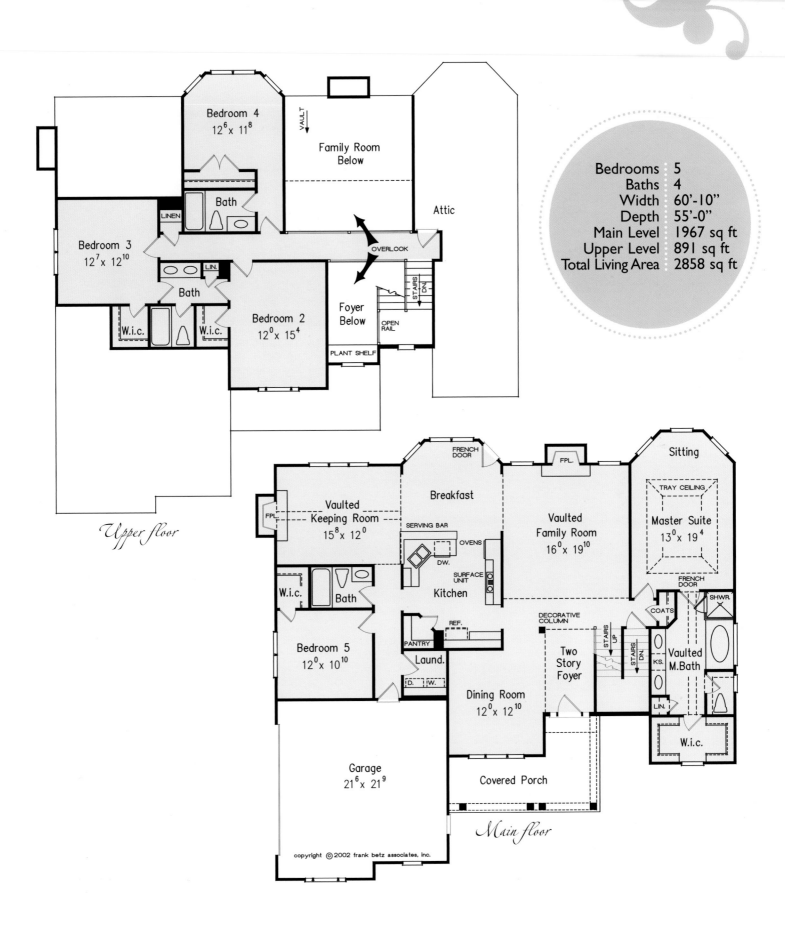

Bedroom 4
12⁶ x 11⁸

Family Room Below

VAULT

Bath

LINEN

Bedroom 3
12⁷ x 12¹⁰

Attic

OVERLOOK

Bath

LIN.

STAIRS DN

Bedroom 2
12⁰ x 15⁴

Foyer Below

OPEN RAIL

PLANT SHELF

W.i.c.    W.i.c.

*Upper floor*

**Bedrooms** 5
**Baths** 4
**Width** 60'-10"
**Depth** 55'-0"
**Main Level** 1967 sq ft
**Upper Level** 891 sq ft
**Total Living Area** 2858 sq ft

FRENCH DOOR

FPL.

Sitting

Breakfast

TRAY CEILING

Vaulted Keeping Room
15⁸ x 12⁰

FPL

SERVING BAR

OVENS

Vaulted Family Room
16⁰ x 19¹⁰

Master Suite
13⁰ x 19⁴

DW.

SURFACE UNIT

FRENCH DOOR

W.i.c.    Bath

Kitchen

SHWR.

COATS

REF.

DECORATIVE COLUMN

STAIRS UP    STAIRS DN

KS.

Vaulted M.Bath

PANTRY

Bedroom 5
12⁰ x 10¹⁰

Laund.

Two Story Foyer

LIN.

D.  W.

Dining Room
12⁰ x 12¹⁰

W.i.c.

Garage
21⁶ x 21⁹

Covered Porch

*Main floor*

copyright © 2002 frank betz associates, inc.

# Candler Park

Plan Number: MLFB04-3777
Price Code: G

A covered front porch gives a warm welcome to guests as they enter the Candler Park. A two-story foyer extends the friendly greeting. A vaulted keeping room – with a fireplace as its backdrop – provides a cozy spot to visit. Accessorizing the dining room will be fun and easy with a furniture niche and decorative columns to work with. A main-floor bedroom makes the perfect nursery with easy access to the master suite. Two bedrooms upstairs enjoy private baths. An optional bonus room is available upstairs as well, making the perfect playroom, exercise area or home office. ■

Foundations Available: Basement, Crawl or Slab

*Rear elevation*

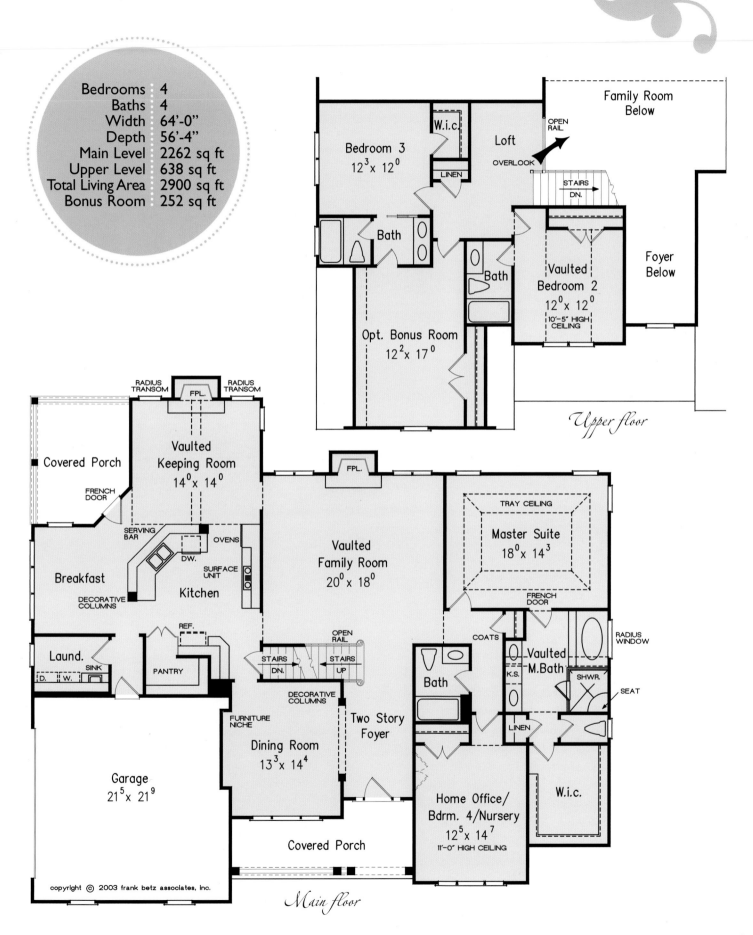

Bedrooms : 4
Baths : 4
Width : 64'-0"
Depth : 56'-4"
Main Level : 2262 sq ft
Upper Level : 638 sq ft
Total Living Area : 2900 sq ft
Bonus Room : 252 sq ft

Family Room Below

W.i.c.

Bedroom 3
$12^3$ x $12^0$

Loft

OPEN RAIL

OVERLOOK

LINEN

STAIRS DN.

Bath

Bath

Vaulted Bedroom 2
$12^0$ x $12^0$
10'-5" HIGH CEILING

Foyer Below

Opt. Bonus Room
$12^2$ x $17^0$

*Upper floor*

RADIUS TRANSOM

FPL.

RADIUS TRANSOM

Vaulted Keeping Room
$14^0$ x $14^0$

FPL.

TRAY CEILING

Covered Porch

FRENCH DOOR

Master Suite
$18^0$ x $14^3$

SERVING BAR

OVENS

Vaulted Family Room
$20^0$ x $18^0$

Breakfast

DW.

SURFACE UNIT

DECORATIVE COLUMNS

Kitchen

FRENCH DOOR

COATS

RADIUS WINDOW

REF.

OPEN RAIL

Vaulted M.Bath

K.S.

Laund.

PANTRY

STAIRS DN.

STAIRS UP

Bath

SHWR.

SEAT

SINK

D. W.

FURNITURE NICHE

DECORATIVE COLUMNS

Two Story Foyer

LINEN

Garage
$21^5$ x $21^9$

Dining Room
$13^3$ x $14^4$

Home Office/ Bdrm. 4/Nursery
$12^5$ x $14^7$
11'-0" HIGH CEILING

W.i.c.

Covered Porch

*Main floor*

# River Forest

Plan Number: MLFB04-3903
Price Code: G

*From the Southern Living® Design Collection* - Stacked stone, board-and-batten accents and carriage doors all contribute to the casually elegant demeanor of the River Forest. Beauty and function are coupled together to create a smart and attractive floor plan inside. A coffered ceiling canopies the family room adding character and dimension to the room. A bench and coat hooks are strategically placed just off the garage, keeping coats and book bags in their place. Three bedrooms – one with a private bath – share the upper level of the home. An optional bonus room is also available upstairs, giving families room to grow when necessary. ■

Foundations Available: Basement or Crawl

*Rear elevation*

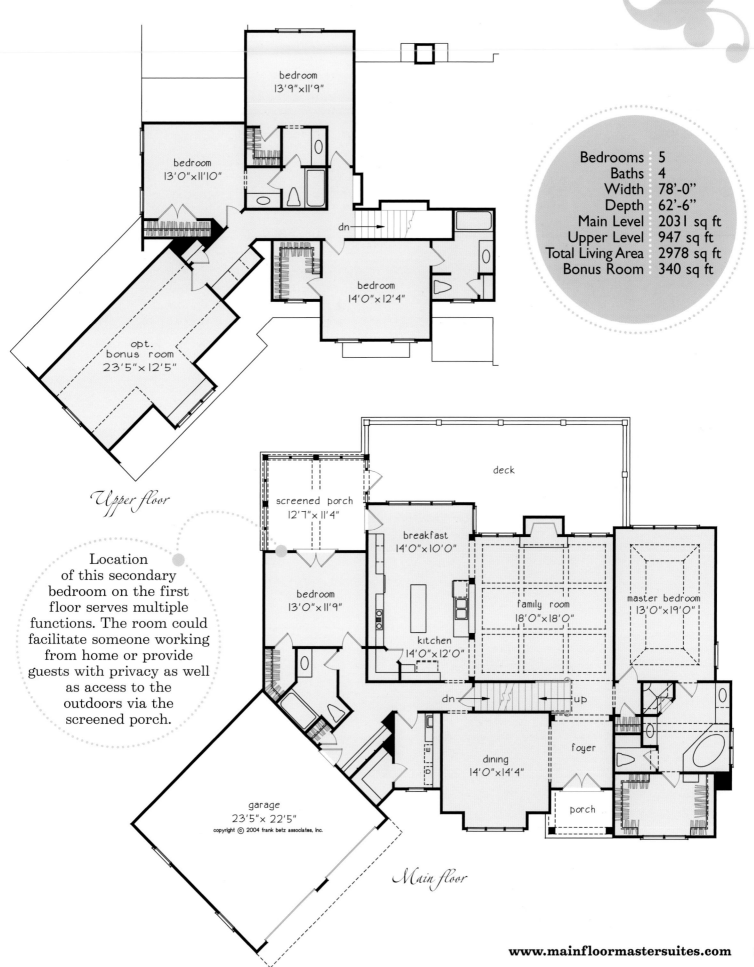

bedroom
13'9"x11'9"

bedroom
13'0"x11'10"

dn

bedroom
14'0"x12'4"

opt.
bonus room
23'5"x12'5"

*Upper floor*

Bedrooms 5
Baths 4
Width 78'-0"
Depth 62'-6"
Main Level 2031 sq ft
Upper Level 947 sq ft
Total Living Area 2978 sq ft
Bonus Room 340 sq ft

Location of this secondary bedroom on the first floor serves multiple functions. The room could facilitate someone working from home or provide guests with privacy as well as access to the outdoors via the screened porch.

deck

screened porch
12'7"x11'4"

breakfast
14'0"x10'0"

bedroom
13'0"x11'9"

kitchen
14'0"x12'0"

family room
18'0"x18'0"

master bedroom
13'0"x19'0"

dn    up

dining
14'0"x14'4"

foyer

porch

garage
23'5"x 22'5"

copyright © 2004 frank betz associates, inc.

*Main floor*

# Montaigne

Plan Number: MLFB04-3731
Price Code: F

Granite-grey shutters, native stone and shingles create the right mix of rugged and refined elements in this rural American classic. A gallery foyer defined by arches and columns grants vistas that extend from the entry to the back property. Twin windows flank a centered fireplace in the family room—a relaxed arena that is suited for elegant planned events and family gatherings. Bay windows in the breakfast area, master suite and an upper-level bedroom invite a sense of nature throughout the home. An entire wing of the home is dedicated to the owners' retreat, with a sitting area. On the upper level, a gallery loft permits views of the keeping room below. ■

Foundations Available: Basement or Crawl

*Rear elevation*

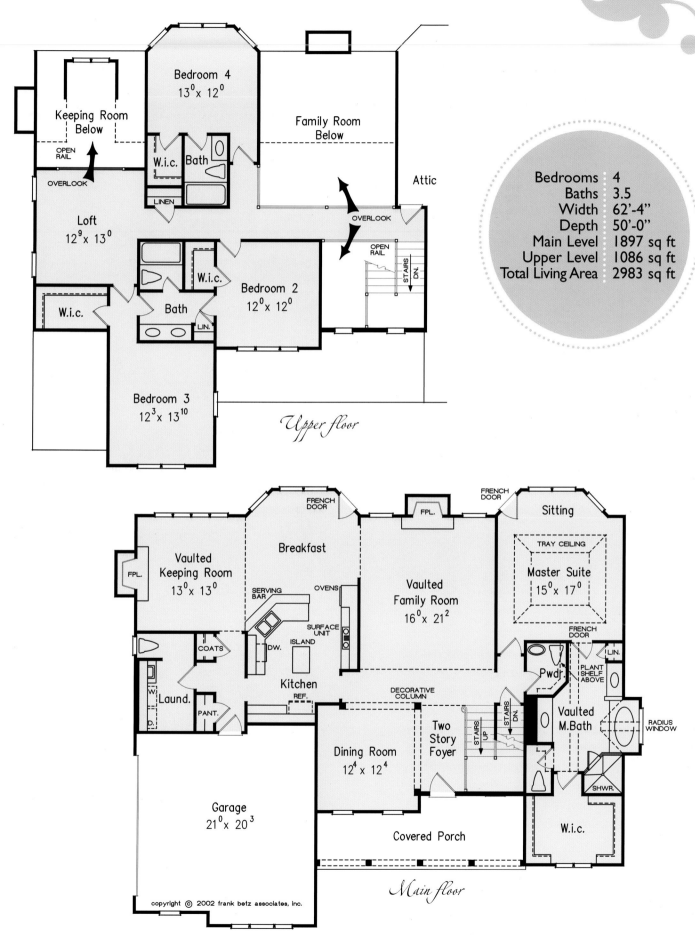

Bedroom 4
13⁰ x 12⁰

Keeping Room Below

OPEN RAIL

OVERLOOK

Family Room Below

Attic

W.i.c.

Bath

LINEN

Loft
12⁹ x 13⁰

OVERLOOK

OPEN RAIL

STAIRS DN.

W.i.c.

Bath

Bedroom 2
12⁰ x 12⁰

W.i.c.

LIN.

Bedroom 3
12³ x 13¹⁰

*Upper floor*

Bedrooms 4
Baths 3.5
Width 62'-4"
Depth 50'-0"
Main Level 1897 sq ft
Upper Level 1086 sq ft
Total Living Area 2983 sq ft

FRENCH DOOR

FPL.

FRENCH DOOR

Sitting

Vaulted Keeping Room
13⁰ x 13⁰

FPL.

Breakfast

SERVING BAR

OVENS

Vaulted Family Room
16⁰ x 21²

TRAY CEILING

Master Suite
15⁰ x 17⁰

FRENCH DOOR

COATS

DW.

SURFACE UNIT

ISLAND

Kitchen

REF.

Pwdr.

LIN.

PLANT SHELF ABOVE

W.

Laund.

PANT.

DECORATIVE COLUMN

Two Story Foyer

STAIRS UP

STAIRS DN.

Vaulted M.Bath

RADIUS WINDOW

Dining Room
12⁴ x 12⁴

SHWR.

Garage
21⁰ x 20³

W.i.c.

Covered Porch

*Main floor*

copyright © 2002 frank betz associates, inc.

# Westhampton

Plan Number: MLFB04-3767
Price Code: G

The distinctive stone exterior of the Westhampton sets the stage for the unique layout inside. A cozy keeping room is situated adjacent to the kitchen, creating uncommon angles. The master suite is secluded on the main level, and features a bayed sitting area — a great spot to unwind. Three additional bedrooms have private access to bathing areas and walk-in closets. A built-in desk is incorporated in the upper floor, giving children a perfect place to do homework or crafts. A third garage bay is separate from the others, providing the perfect spot for a boat or utility storage. ∎

Foundations Available: Basement or Crawl

*Rear elevation*

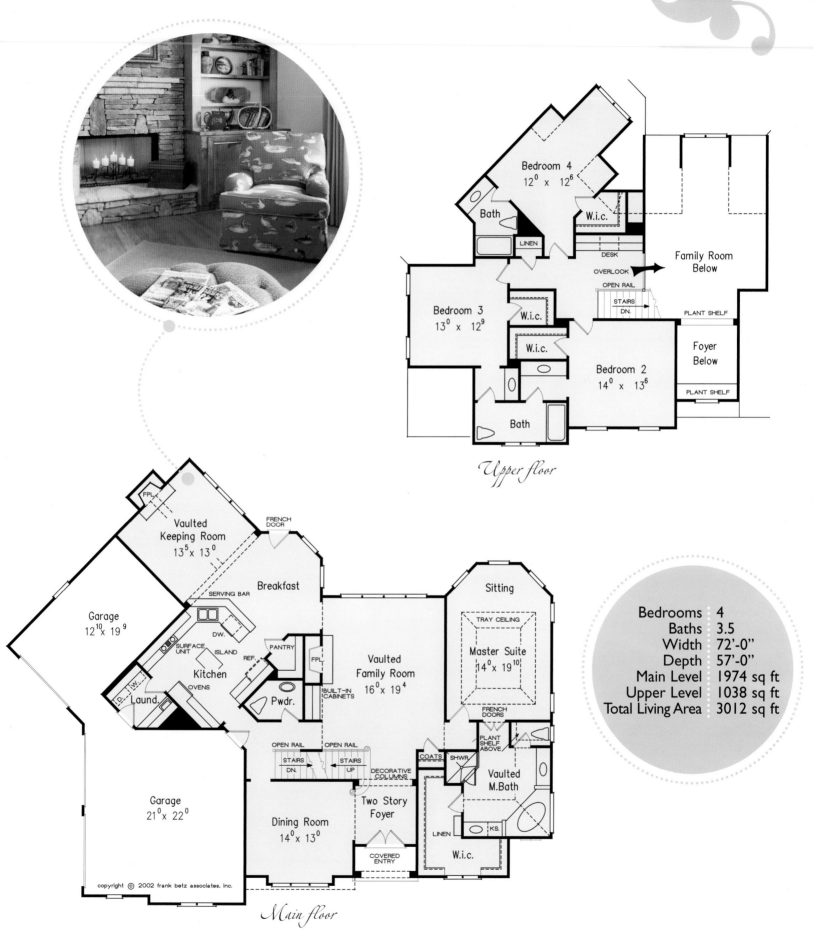

Bedroom 4
$12^0$ x $12^6$

Bath

LINEN

W.i.c.

DESK

Family Room Below

OVERLOOK

OPEN RAIL

Bedroom 3
$13^0$ x $12^9$

W.i.c.

STAIRS DN.

PLANT SHELF

W.i.c.

Foyer Below

Bedroom 2
$14^0$ x $13^6$

PLANT SHELF

Bath

*Upper floor*

FPL

Vaulted Keeping Room
$13^5$ x $13^0$

FRENCH DOOR

Breakfast

SERVING BAR

Sitting

Garage
$12^{10}$ x $19^9$

SURFACE UNIT

DW.

ISLAND

PANTRY

REF.

FPL

TRAY CEILING

Master Suite
$14^0$ x $19^{10}$

Kitchen

OVENS

BUILT-IN CABINETS

Vaulted Family Room
$16^0$ x $19^4$

D. W.

Laund.

Pwdr.

FRENCH DOORS

OPEN RAIL

OPEN RAIL

COATS

PLANT SHELF ABOVE

STAIRS DN.

STAIRS UP

DECORATIVE COLUMNS

SHWR

Vaulted M.Bath

Garage
$21^0$ x $22^0$

Two Story Foyer

LINEN

KS.

Dining Room
$14^0$ x $13^0$

W.i.c.

copyright © 2002 frank betz associates, inc.

COVERED ENTRY

*Main floor*

Bedrooms 4
Baths 3.5
Width 72'-0"
Depth 57'-0"
Main Level 1974 sq ft
Upper Level 1038 sq ft
Total Living Area 3012 sq ft

# Northampton

Plan Number: MLFB04-1005
Price Code: G

Innovative design details are apparent throughout the Northampton. Its façade features a turret and a terrace area, giving it phenomenal curb appeal. The dining room is defined by architectural columns, keeping this space open and accessible to the rest of the main floor. The room with a turret makes a beautiful study, but can be easily altered to make a stunning sitting area for the master bedroom. The kitchen overlooks a vaulted keeping room. Its fireplace makes it a cozy place to end the day. Optional bonus space is available on the second floor, allowing the homeowners to finish it as they wish. ■

Foundations Available: Basement, Crawl or Slab

*Rear elevation*

Family Room Below

RADIUS WINDOW

W.i.c.

LINEN

Bedroom 3
14⁰ x 12⁰

OPEN RAIL

OVERLOOK

NICHE

STAIRS DN.

PLANT SHELF ABOVE

W.i.c.

Foyer Below

Bedroom 2
13⁰ x 12⁹
11'-0" HIGH CEILING

Bath

K.S.

Bath

W.i.c.

PLANT SHELF

Opt.
Bonus Room
12⁵ x 22⁹

*Upper floor*

RADIUS WINDOW

K.S.

Hers

MIRROR

Vaulted M.Bath

PLANT SHELF ABOVE

SHWR. SEAT

His

LINEN

FRENCH DOORS

RAD. WDW.

FPL.

RAD. WDW.

VAULT

VAULT

Vaulted Keeping Room
13⁵ x 14³

FRENCH DOOR

FRENCH DOOR

TRAY CEILING

Pwdr.

Master Suite
16⁰ x 19⁰

TRAY CLG.

ARCHED OPENING

Two Story Family Room
18⁸ x 18⁴

DESK

K.S.

FPL.

PANTRY

COATS

Breakfast

ISLAND

SURFACE UNIT

DW.

STAIRS DN.

ARCHED OPENINGS

OPEN RAIL

STAIRS UP

Dining Room
13⁰ x 16⁶

D.

W.

Laund.

SINK

Kitchen

REF.

DBL. OVEN

BOOKSHELVES

Sitting Room/ Den
14⁰ x 14⁸

FRENCH DOORS

Two Story Foyer

TRAY CLG.

Terrace

Three Car Garage
20⁶ x 30³

*Main floor*

Bedrooms : 3
Baths : 3.5
Width : 63'-6"
Depth : 71'-4"
Main Level : 2429 sq ft
Upper Level : 654 sq ft
Total Living Area : 3083 sq ft
Bonus Room : 420 sq ft

copyright © 1996 frank betz associates, inc.

# Waterman

Plan Number: MLFB04-3907
Price Code: E

Lattice accents and three dormers accent the exterior of the Waterman design. Its cottage-style appeal is friendly and welcoming, with a covered front porch to greet guests and homeowners. Its kitchen, breakfast area and keeping room gently combine into one common space, making it the center point of the home where family and friends gather. Radius windows in the family room let plenty of sunshine in. Decorative art niches line the stairway to the upper level creating great decorating opportunities. The entertainment room upstairs gives children their own designated space to play games or spend time with friends. ▪

Foundations Available: Basement, Crawl or Slab

*Rear elevation*

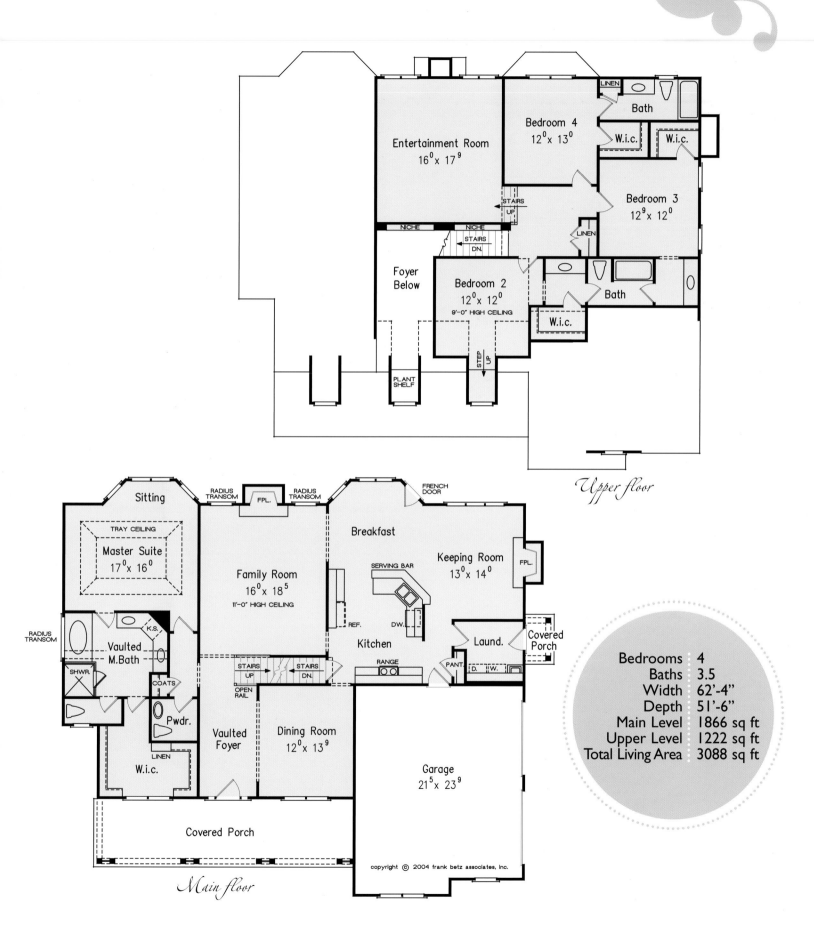

*Upper floor*

*Main floor*

Sitting

TRAY CEILING

Master Suite
17⁰ x 16⁰

RADIUS
TRANSOM

FPL.

RADIUS
TRANSOM

RADIUS
TRANSOM

FRENCH
DOOR

Breakfast

Keeping Room
13⁰ x 14⁰

FPL

Family Room
16⁰ x 18⁵
11'-0" HIGH CEILING

SERVING BAR

K.S.

Vaulted
M.Bath

REF.

DW.

Kitchen

Laund.

Covered
Porch

SHWR.

COATS

STAIRS
UP

STAIRS
DN.

RANGE

PANT.

D. W.

OPEN
RAIL

Pwdr.

LINEN

Vaulted
Foyer

Dining Room
12⁰ x 13⁹

W.i.c.

Garage
21⁵ x 23⁹

Covered Porch

copyright © 2004 frank betz associates, inc.

Entertainment Room
16⁰ x 17⁹

Bedroom 4
12⁰ x 13⁰

LINEN

Bath

W.i.c.

W.i.c.

Bedroom 3
12⁹ x 12⁰

STAIRS
UP

NICHE

NICHE

STAIRS
DN.

LINEN

Foyer
Below

Bedroom 2
12⁰ x 12⁰
9'-0" HIGH CEILING

Bath

W.i.c.

STEP
UP

PLANT
SHELF

| Bedrooms | 4 |
| Baths | 3.5 |
| Width | 62'-4" |
| Depth | 51'-6" |
| Main Level | 1866 sq ft |
| Upper Level | 1222 sq ft |
| Total Living Area | 3088 sq ft |

# Muirfield

Plan Number: MLFB04-3769
Price Code: G

The lifestyle of today's growing family has brought new demands on home design. The Muirfield is the result of careful consideration of these needs. The kitchen, breakfast area and vaulted keeping room come together to create a unified space for casual family time. His-and-her closets and a lavish master bath create a "suite" spot to start and end your day. The second-floor bedrooms all feature walk-in closets and bath access – a rarity in today's designs. A built-in desk in the second-floor loft creates the perfect homework station for kids. The three-car garage has one secluded bay, ideal for lawn and garden storage, a boat or RV. ■

Foundations Available: Basement or Crawl

*Rear elevation*

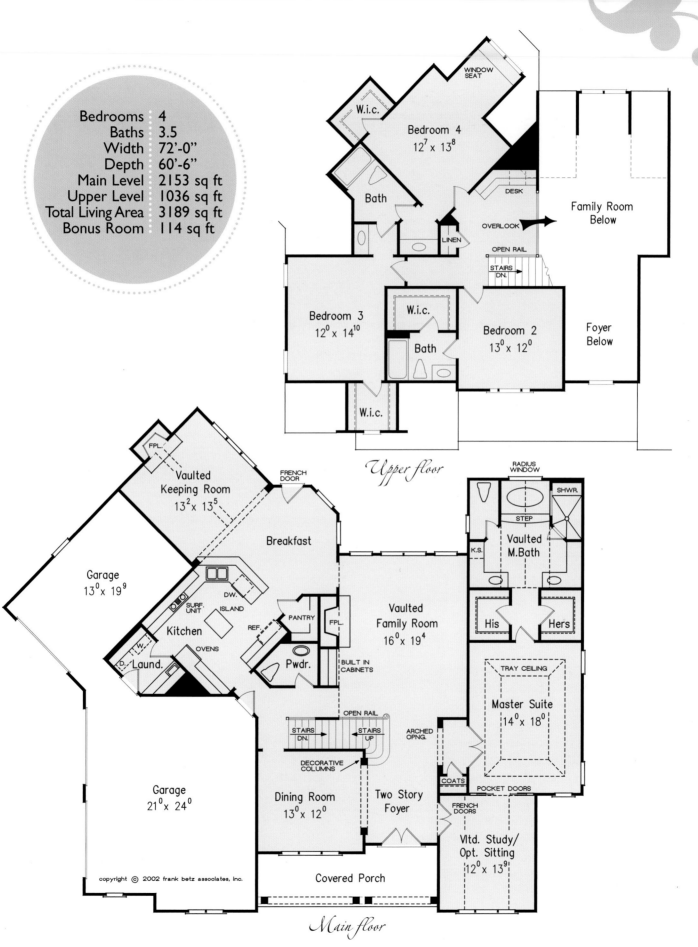

Bedrooms | 4
Baths | 3.5
Width | 72'-0"
Depth | 60'-6"
Main Level | 2153 sq ft
Upper Level | 1036 sq ft
Total Living Area | 3189 sq ft
Bonus Room | 114 sq ft

*Upper floor*

*Main floor*

# Forrest Hills

Plan Number: MLFB04-3802
Price Code: F

Traditional elements join forces on the façade of the Forrest Hills to add relaxed and charming curb appeal to its streetscape. Copper accents and a cupola atop the garage are special details that make this house feel like home. Multiple gathering spaces inside give families plenty of choices on where to spend their time. A keeping room just off the kitchen is a great place for reconnecting at the end of a busy day. The family room – complete with a fireplace and built-in cabinetry – makes a cozy retreat for evenings in front of the fire. An entertainment room upstairs gives children a designated place to spend their recreational time.

Foundations Available: Basement or Crawl

*Rear elevation*

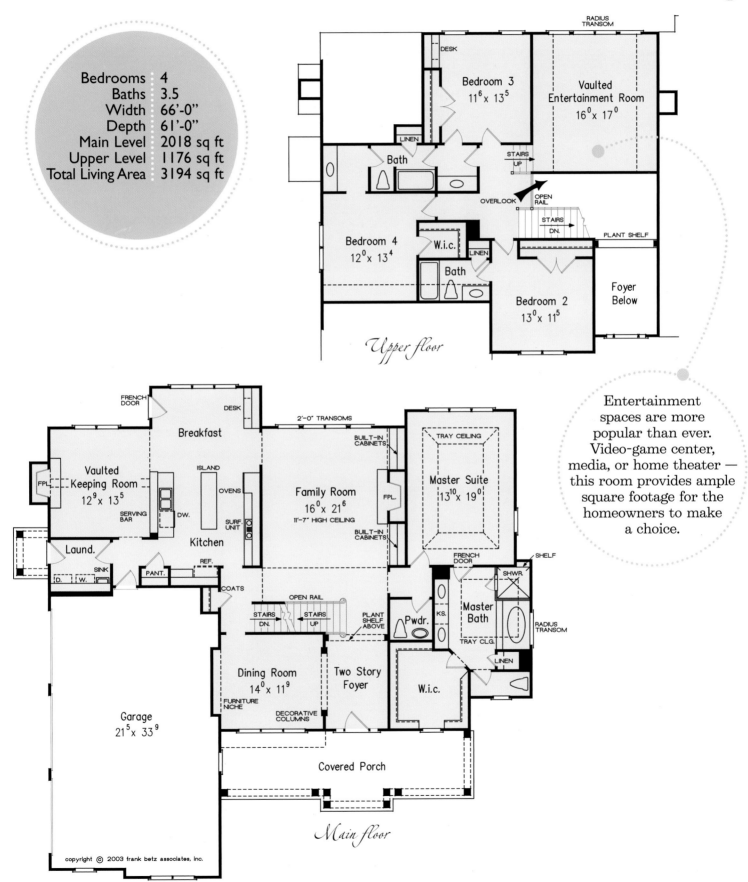

Bedrooms | 4
Baths | 3.5
Width | 66'-0"
Depth | 61'-0"
Main Level | 2018 sq ft
Upper Level | 1176 sq ft
Total Living Area | 3194 sq ft

*Upper floor*

Entertainment spaces are more popular than ever. Video-game center, media, or home theater — this room provides ample square footage for the homeowners to make a choice.

*Main floor*

copyright © 2003 frank betz associates, inc.

# McGinnis Ferry

Plan Number: MLFB04-3879
Price Code: F

One glance and you'll see what Old World style is all about. Fieldstone accents against board-and-batten siding generate the welcoming and warm appeal that Old World homes are known for. A vaulted keeping room connects to the kitchen and breakfast areas, creating that relaxing place to rest and unwind. Transom and radius windows illuminate the main floor with plenty of natural light. A mudroom and coat closet are placed just off the garage, routing traffic through it before entering the rest of the home. A teen suite has been designed into the second floor near the bedrooms. Equipped with a built-in desk, this spot makes the perfect homework station and recreational hang-out. ■

Foundations Available: Basement or Crawl

*Rear elevation*

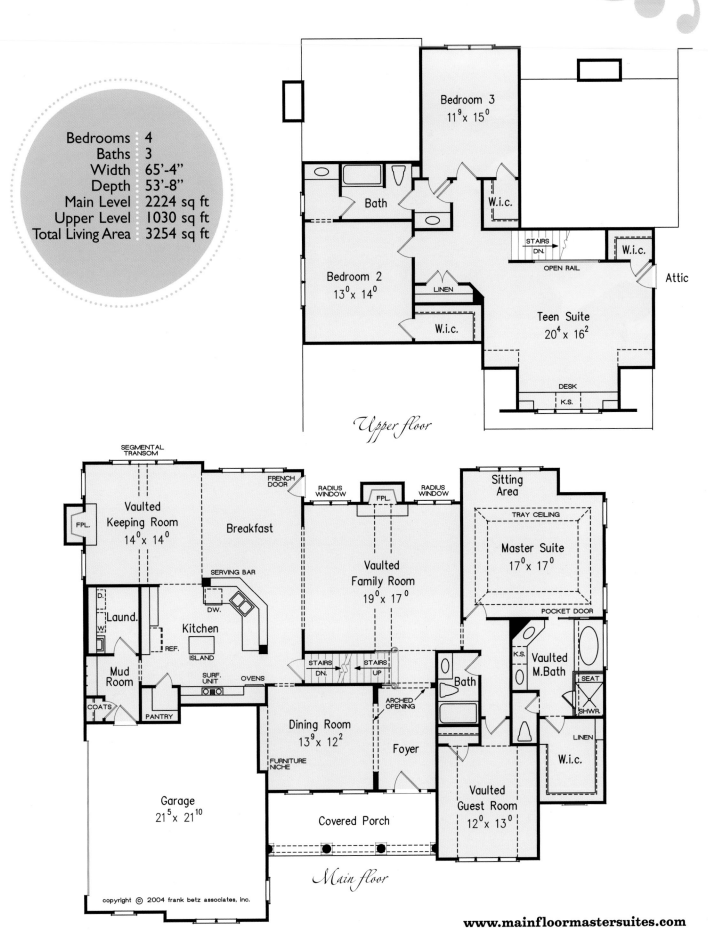

Bedrooms : 4
Baths : 3
Width : 65'-4"
Depth : 53'-8"
Main Level : 2224 sq ft
Upper Level : 1030 sq ft
Total Living Area : 3254 sq ft

**Bedroom 3**
$11^9$ x $15^0$

Bath

W.i.c.

W.i.c.

Attic

STAIRS DN.

OPEN RAIL

**Bedroom 2**
$13^0$ x $14^0$

LINEN

W.i.c.

**Teen Suite**
$20^4$ x $16^2$

DESK

K.S.

*Upper floor*

SEGMENTAL TRANSOM

FRENCH DOOR

RADIUS WINDOW

FPL.

RADIUS WINDOW

**Sitting Area**

FPL.

**Vaulted Keeping Room**
$14^0$ x $14^0$

**Breakfast**

TRAY CEILING

**Master Suite**
$17^0$ x $17^0$

SERVING BAR

**Vaulted Family Room**
$19^0$ x $17^0$

DW.

D.

Laund.

W.

**Kitchen**

REF.

ISLAND

**Mud Room**

SURF. UNIT

OVENS

STAIRS DN.

STAIRS UP

Bath

POCKET DOOR

K.S.

**Vaulted M.Bath**

SEAT

SHWR.

COATS

PANTRY

ARCHED OPENING

LINEN

**Dining Room**
$13^9$ x $12^2$

**Foyer**

W.i.c.

FURNITURE NICHE

**Garage**
$21^5$ x $21^{10}$

**Vaulted Guest Room**
$12^0$ x $13^0$

**Covered Porch**

*Main floor*

# Fenway

Plan Number: MLFB04-3444
Price Code: G

Fieldstone accents with board-and-batten shutters create that warm, cottage-like façade that is so popular today. A fire-lit keeping room borders the kitchen and breakfast area, providing the ideal setting for casual gatherings. Sunshine pours in through transom windows in the grand room. A buffet table or china cabinet will fit perfectly into the furniture niche in the dining room. A laundry room with a handy sink provides a second side entrance to the home – ideal for the family's use. Private lounging space has been incorporated into the master suite, giving homeowners a tranquil spot to start and end their days. Three bedrooms upstairs have direct access to bathing areas. ■

Foundations Available: Basement, Crawl or Slab

*Rear elevation*

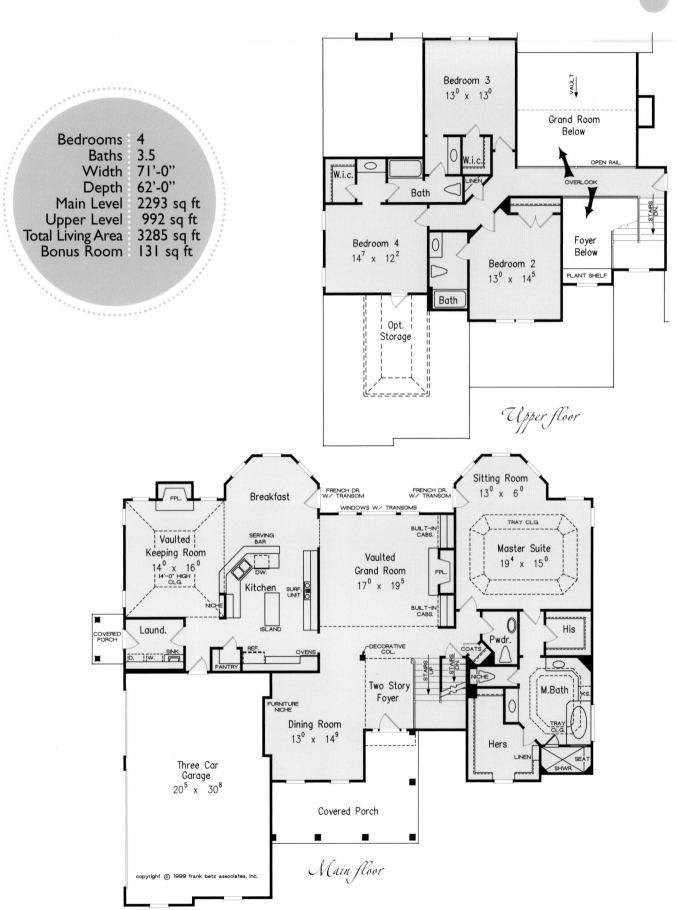

Bedrooms : 4
Baths : 3.5
Width : 71'-0"
Depth : 62'-0"
Main Level : 2293 sq ft
Upper Level : 992 sq ft
Total Living Area : 3285 sq ft
Bonus Room : 131 sq ft

*Upper floor*

*Main floor*

copyright © 1999 frank betz associates, inc.

# Woodcliffe

Plan Number: MLFB04-3757
Price Code: G

Casual elegance describes the Woodcliffe, with its timber-accented gables and a cupola and weather vane atop the garage. Coffered ceilings create interesting dimension throughout the main level of this home. Art niches are designed at the top of the staircase providing innovative decorating opportunities. The master suite has a quiet sitting area with views to the backyard. A large family recreation room is incorporated into the upper level, providing flexible options like a media room or exercise area. An enormous optional bonus room on the upper level gives the homeowner even more choices, suitable for a playroom or home office. ■

Foundations Available: Basement or Crawl

*Rear elevation*

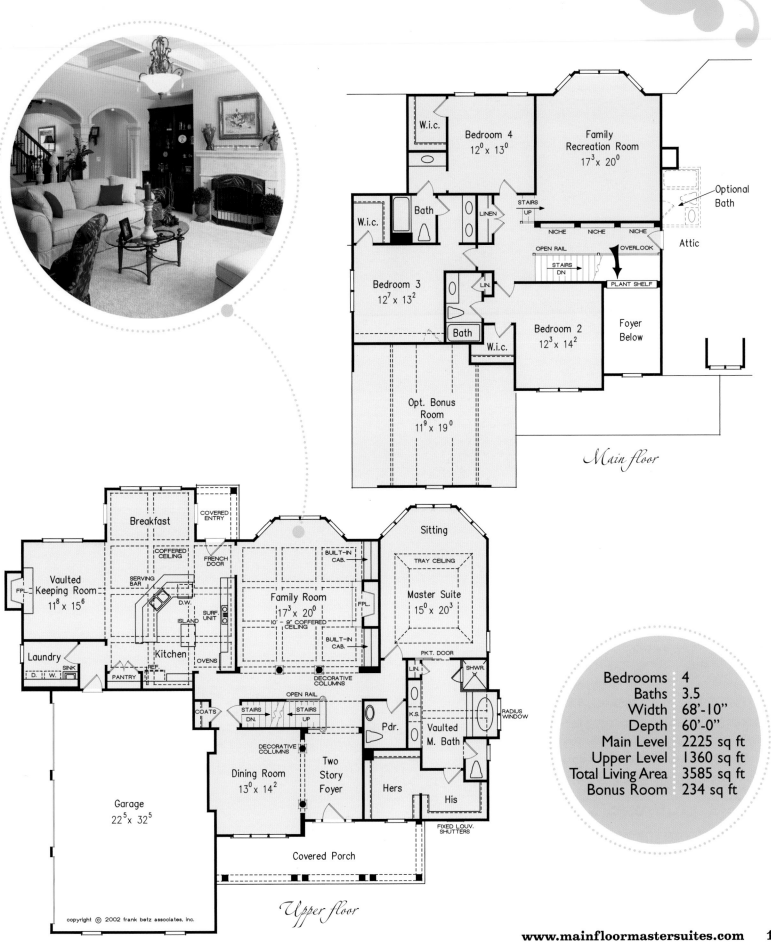

**Main floor**

- W.i.c.
- Bedroom 4 — 12⁰ x 13⁰
- Family Recreation Room — 17³ x 20⁰
- Optional Bath
- Attic
- Bath
- LINEN
- STAIRS UP
- NICHE NICHE NICHE
- OPEN RAIL
- OVERLOOK
- W.i.c.
- Bedroom 3 — 12⁷ x 13²
- LIN.
- STAIRS DN
- PLANT SHELF
- Bath
- Bedroom 2 — 12³ x 14²
- Foyer Below
- W.i.c.
- Opt. Bonus Room — 11⁹ x 19⁰

**Upper floor**

- Breakfast
- COVERED ENTRY
- COFFERED CEILING
- FRENCH DOOR
- BUILT-IN CAB.
- Sitting
- TRAY CEILING
- Vaulted Keeping Room — 11⁸ x 15⁶
- SERVING BAR
- D.W.
- ISLAND
- SURF. UNIT
- Family Room — 17³ x 20⁰ — 10' - 9" COFFERED CEILING
- FPL.
- Master Suite — 15⁰ x 20³
- Laundry
- D. W. SINK
- PANTRY
- REF.
- Kitchen
- OVENS
- BUILT-IN CAB.
- DECORATIVE COLUMNS
- PKT. DOOR
- LIN.
- SHWR.
- COATS
- STAIRS DN
- OPEN RAIL
- STAIRS UP
- Pdr.
- K.S.
- Vaulted M. Bath
- RADIUS WINDOW
- DECORATIVE COLUMNS
- Dining Room — 13⁰ x 14²
- Two Story Foyer
- Hers
- His
- Garage — 22⁵ x 32⁵
- FIXED LOUV. SHUTTERS
- Covered Porch

| Bedrooms | 4 |
|---|---|
| Baths | 3.5 |
| Width | 68'-10" |
| Depth | 60'-0" |
| Main Level | 2225 sq ft |
| Upper Level | 1360 sq ft |
| Total Living Area | 3585 sq ft |
| Bonus Room | 234 sq ft |

# Greywell

Plan Number: MLFB04-3914
Price Code: G

Beam-accented gables with board-and-batten accents give the Greywell that cozy cottage-like curb appeal that homeowners are seeking today. One step inside and it's easy to see that its character doesn't stop at the curb. The kitchen overlooks a gracious breakfast area, as well as a fire-lit keeping room, providing plenty of space for family time or entertaining. A screened porch is accessed off this area as well providing the perfect opportunity to take the party outside. Coffered ceilings and built-in cabinetry make the family room extra special. A children's retreat upstairs makes the perfect playroom or can be easily used as a fourth bedroom or guest suite. ▪

Foundations Available: Basement or Crawl

*Rear elevation*

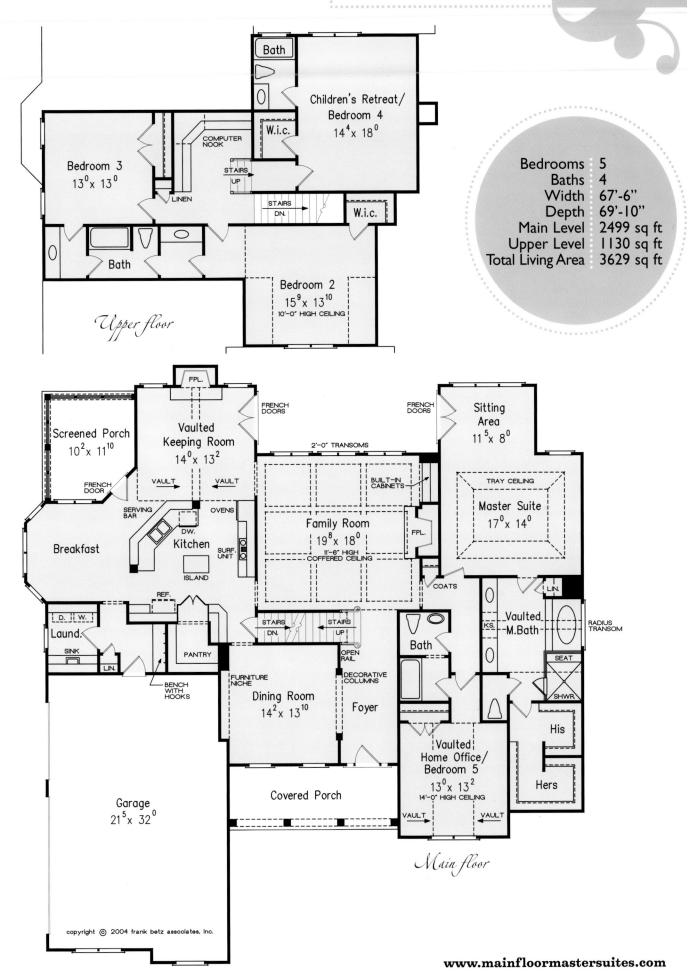

**Bath**

**Children's Retreat/
Bedroom 4**
14⁴ x 18⁰

COMPUTER
NOOK

W.i.c.

**Bedroom 3**
13⁰ x 13⁰

STAIRS
UP

LINEN

STAIRS
DN.

W.i.c.

Bath

**Bedroom 2**
15⁹ x 13¹⁰
10'-0" HIGH CEILING

*Upper floor*

Bedrooms | 5
Baths | 4
Width | 67'-6"
Depth | 69'-10"
Main Level | 2499 sq ft
Upper Level | 1130 sq ft
Total Living Area | 3629 sq ft

FPL.

FRENCH
DOORS

FRENCH
DOORS

**Sitting
Area**
11⁵ x 8⁰

**Screened Porch**
10² x 11¹⁰

**Vaulted
Keeping Room**
14⁰ x 13²

2'-0" TRANSOMS

TRAY CEILING

FRENCH
DOOR

VAULT

VAULT

BUILT-IN
CABINETS

**Master Suite**
17⁰ x 14⁰

SERVING
BAR

OVENS

**Family Room**
19⁸ x 18⁰
11'-6" HIGH
COFFERED CEILING

FPL.

DW.

**Breakfast**

**Kitchen**

SURF.
UNIT

ISLAND

COATS

RADIUS
TRANSOM

KS.

**Vaulted
M.Bath**

REF.

SEAT

D. W.

**Laund.**

SINK

LIN.

PANTRY

STAIRS
DN.

STAIRS
UP

OPEN
RAIL

**Bath**

SHWR.

**His**

BENCH
WITH
HOOKS

FURNITURE
NICHE

DECORATIVE
COLUMNS

**Hers**

**Dining Room**
14² x 13¹⁰

**Foyer**

**Vaulted
Home Office/
Bedroom 5**
13⁰ x 13²
14'-0" HIGH CEILING

**Garage**
21⁵ x 32⁰

**Covered Porch**

VAULT

VAULT

*Main floor*

# Greyhawk

Plan Number: MLFB04-3479
Price Code: G

Stately brick and clapboard siding are a welcome combination in neighborhoods new and old. They come together on the Greyhawk to create an established-looking yet modern front elevation. Some of today's latest and greatest progressive amenities have been incorporated into its floor plan. The kitchen is situated at a unique angle, adding an interesting dimension to the main floor. It overlooks a breakfast area and keeping room that unite to create a casual, comfortable place for families to spend quality time. An arched opening and built-in cabinetry in the family room are special details that make this home unique. ■

Foundations Available: Basement, Crawl or Slab

*Rear elevation*

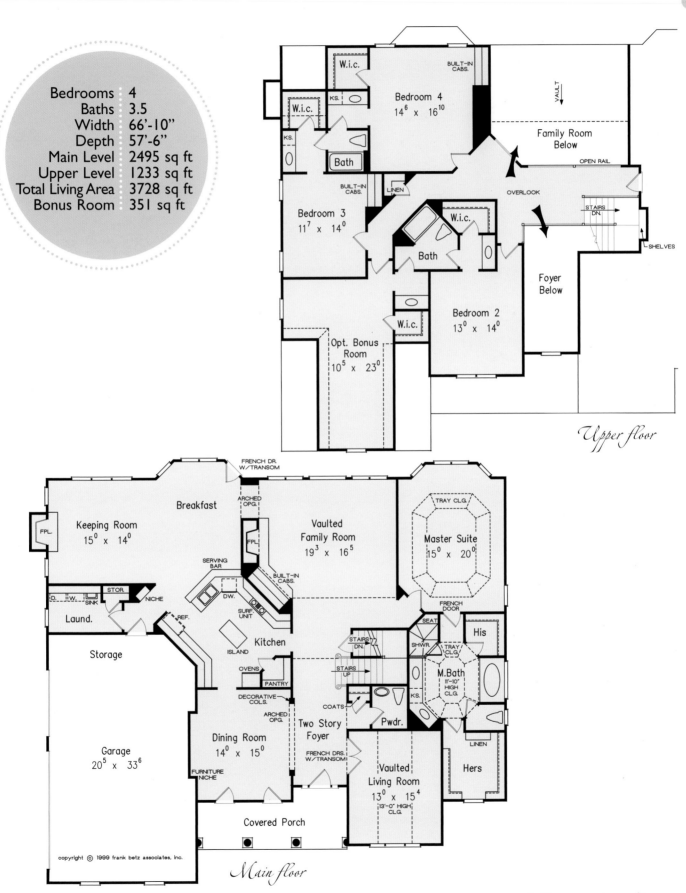

Bedrooms 4
Baths 3.5
Width 66'-10"
Depth 57'-6"
Main Level 2495 sq ft
Upper Level 1233 sq ft
Total Living Area 3728 sq ft
Bonus Room 351 sq ft

W.i.c.

BUILT-IN CABS.

Bedroom 4
14⁶ x 16¹⁰

VAULT

KS.

W.i.c.

Family Room Below

KS.

OPEN RAIL

Bath

OVERLOOK

STAIRS DN.

BUILT-IN CABS.

LINEN

SHELVES

Bedroom 3
11⁷ x 14⁰

W.i.c.

Bath

Foyer Below

W.i.c.

Bedroom 2
13⁰ x 14⁰

Opt. Bonus Room
10⁵ x 23⁰

*Upper floor*

FRENCH DR. W/TRANSOM

Breakfast

ARCHED OPG.

Vaulted Family Room
19³ x 16⁵

TRAY CLG.

Master Suite
15⁰ x 20⁰

FPL.

Keeping Room
15⁰ x 14⁰

FPL.

SERVING BAR

BUILT-IN CABS.

FRENCH DOOR

D. W. SINK

STOR.

NICHE

DW.

SURF. UNIT

SEAT

His

Laund.

REF.

Kitchen

STAIRS DN.

SHWR.

TRAY CLG.

Storage

ISLAND

STAIRS UP

KS.

M.Bath
11'-10" HIGH CLG.

OVENS

DECORATIVE COLS.

PANTRY

COATS

Garage
20⁵ x 33⁶

ARCHED OPG.

Two Story Foyer

Pwdr.

LINEN

FURNITURE NICHE

Dining Room
14⁰ x 15⁰

FRENCH DRS. W/TRANSOM

Vaulted Living Room
13⁰ x 15⁴
13'-0" HIGH CLG.

Hers

Covered Porch

*Main floor*

# Baldwin Farm

Plan Number: MLFB04-3831
Price Code: G

*From the Southern Living® Design Collection* - Special accents borrowed from years gone by make the Baldwin Farm feel established and traditional. The carriage doors and cupola on the garage go back in time to add historic elegance to the façade of this home. Some of today's most popular design trends are incorporated inside. The kitchen overlooks a cozy keeping room that adjoins a screened porch and deck — great for entertaining and relaxation. A mudroom is strategically situated inside the secondary entrance, keeping shoes and coats in their place. The second level of the home features a vaulted family entertainment room. Whether playing games, watching television, or exercising, this is a spot where the whole family can enjoy its recreational time. ∎

Foundations Available: Basement, Crawl or Slab

*Rear elevation*

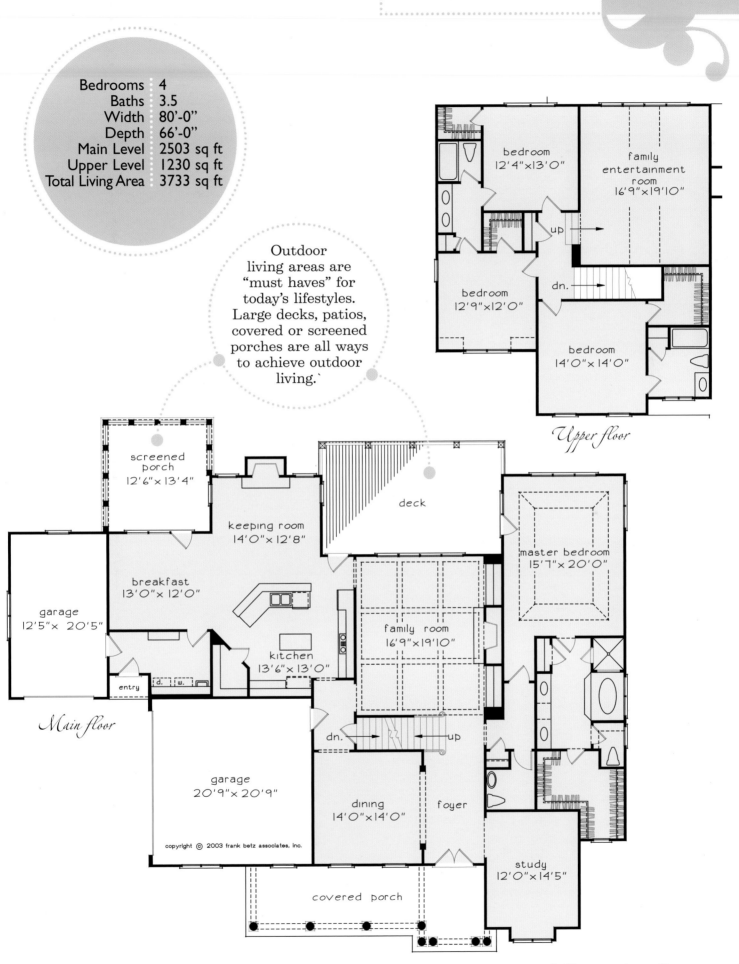

Bedrooms | 4
Baths | 3.5
Width | 80'-0"
Depth | 66'-0"
Main Level | 2503 sq ft
Upper Level | 1230 sq ft
Total Living Area | 3733 sq ft

Outdoor living areas are "must haves" for today's lifestyles. Large decks, patios, covered or screened porches are all ways to achieve outdoor living.`

bedroom
12'4"×13'0"

family entertainment room
16'9"×19'10"

bedroom
12'9"×12'0"

up

dn.

bedroom
14'0"×14'0"

*Upper floor*

screened porch
12'6"×13'4"

keeping room
14'0"×12'8"

deck

master bedroom
15'7"×20'0"

breakfast
13'0"×12'0"

garage
12'5"× 20'5"

kitchen
13'6"×13'0"

family room
16'9"×19'10"

entry

d.  w.

*Main floor*

garage
20'9"×20'9"

dn.

up

dining
14'0"×14'0"

foyer

study
12'0"×14'5"

copyright © 2003 frank betz associates, inc.

covered porch

# Keheley Ridge

Plan Number: MLFB04-3853
Price Code: H

*From the Southern Living® Design Collection -* The warm and friendly exterior of the Keheley Ridge was created by combining stone and siding with unique features, such as board-and-batten shutters and carriage doors. This thoughtful grouping creates a façade that has the Old World charm that so many homeowners are seeking. Continuing with this trend of warmth and comfort, a cozy keeping room with a fireplace is situated off the breakfast area. The entertainer will love the butler's pantry that connects the kitchen and dining room. Each bedroom upstairs enjoys the privacy of personal bathing areas. A family recreation room is designed into the second level, creating the ideal place for casual family fun time. ▪

Foundations Available: Basement or Crawl

*Rear elevation*

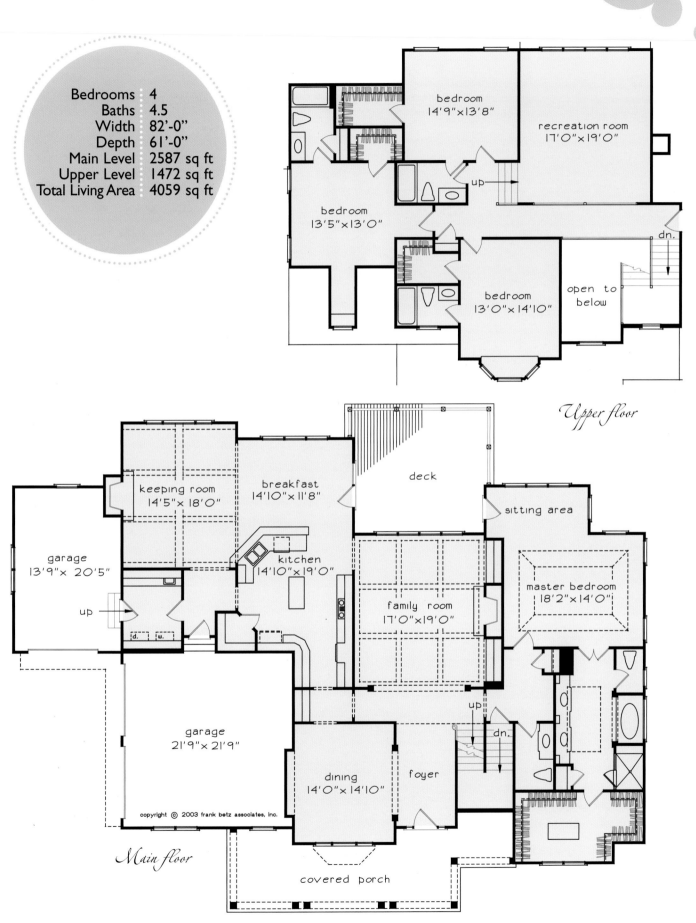

Bedrooms | 4
Baths | 4.5
Width | 82'-0"
Depth | 61'-0"
Main Level | 2587 sq ft
Upper Level | 1472 sq ft
Total Living Area | 4059 sq ft

bedroom
14'9"x13'8"

recreation room
17'0"x19'0"

up

bedroom
13'5"x13'0"

dn.

bedroom
13'0"x14'10"

open to below

*Upper floor*

keeping room
14'5"x 18'0"

breakfast
14'10"x 11'8"

deck

sitting area

garage
13'9"x 20'5"

kitchen
14'10"x 19'0"

master bedroom
18'2"x14'0"

up

d. w.

family room
17'0"x 19'0"

garage
21'9"x 21'9"

up

dn.

dining
14'0"x 14'10"

foyer

copyright © 2003 frank betz associates, inc.

*Main floor*

covered porch

# Clarendon

Plan Number: MLFB04-3685
Price Code: H

Soaring white columns against striking red brick create a time-honored façade that takes you back to yesteryear. The grandeur continues as you step inside the Clarendon. An impressive foyer has a curved staircase and furniture niche. A library – with a massive wall of bookshelves – overlooks the entry. The well-appointed kitchen overlooks a breakfast area, two-story keeping room and covered porch making this space an entertainers dream! A rear foyer adjoins a combination mud and laundry room, providing the ideal spot for daily comings and goings. The lap of luxury awaits you in the master suite, with a dual-entry walk-in shower and private sitting area. ∎

Foundations Available: Basement or Crawl

*Rear elevation*

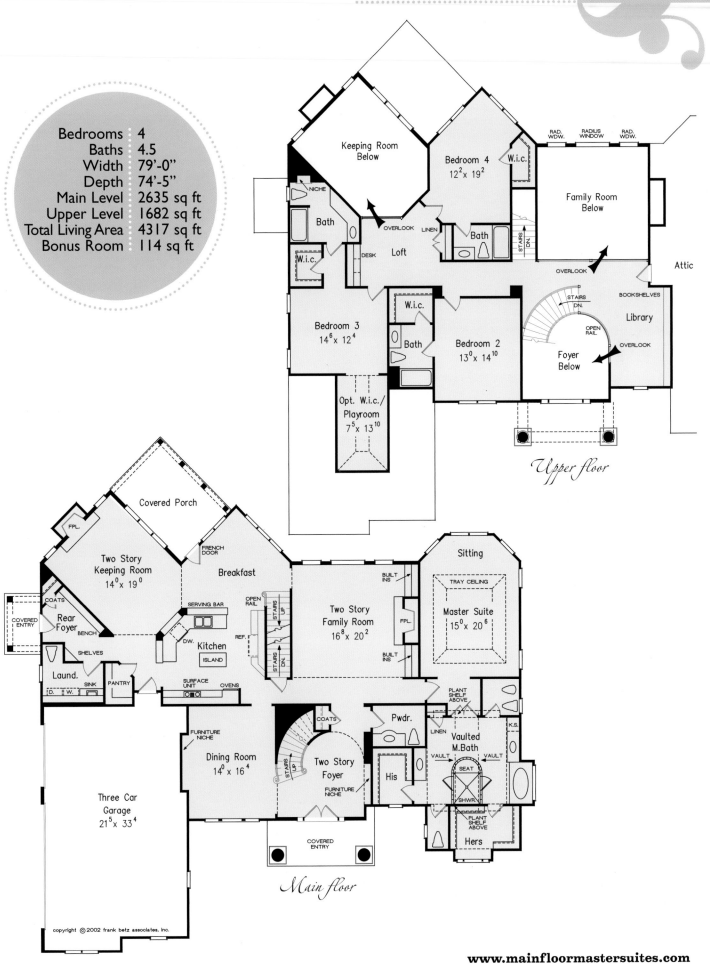

Bedrooms  4
Baths  4.5
Width  79'-0"
Depth  74'-5"
Main Level  2635 sq ft
Upper Level  1682 sq ft
Total Living Area  4317 sq ft
Bonus Room  114 sq ft

Keeping Room Below

Bedroom 4
$12^2$ x $19^2$

W.i.c.

RAD. WDW.   RADIUS WINDOW   RAD. WDW.

Family Room Below

NICHE

Bath

OVERLOOK   LINEN

Bath

STAIRS DN.

W.i.c.

DESK   Loft

OVERLOOK

Attic

Bedroom 3
$14^6$ x $12^4$

W.i.c.

Bath

Bedroom 2
$13^0$ x $14^{10}$

STAIRS DN.

OPEN RAIL

BOOKSHELVES

Library

Foyer Below

OVERLOOK

Opt. W.i.c./ Playroom
$7^5$ x $13^{10}$

*Upper floor*

Covered Porch

FPL.

FRENCH DOOR

Two Story Keeping Room
$14^0$ x $19^0$

Breakfast

Sitting

TRAY CEILING

Master Suite
$15^0$ x $20^6$

COATS

COVERED ENTRY

Rear Foyer

BENCH

SERVING BAR

DW.   Kitchen

ISLAND

REF.

OPEN RAIL

STAIRS UP

Two Story Family Room
$16^8$ x $20^2$

BUILT INS

FPL.

BUILT INS

SHELVES

Laund.

SINK   PANTRY

D. W.

SURFACE UNIT

OVENS

STAIRS UP/DN

PLANT SHELF ABOVE

LINEN

Vaulted M.Bath

K.S.

FURNITURE NICHE

Dining Room
$14^0$ x $16^4$

STAIRS UP

COATS

Pwdr.

Two Story Foyer

His

VAULT   SEAT   VAULT

SHWR.

Three Car Garage
$21^5$ x $33^4$

FURNITURE NICHE

PLANT SHELF ABOVE

Hers

COVERED ENTRY

*Main floor*

copyright © 2002 frank betz associates, inc.

# Castlegate

Plan Number: MLFB04- 790
Price Code: H

Your castle awaits…..A portico entry leads into a breathtaking two-story foyer with a curved staircase. The master suite is appropriately named, with its vaulted sitting room and luxurious bath. A barrel-vaulted ceiling canopies the bath, perfectly appointed with a seated shower and step-up soaking tub. An art niche, built-in cabinetry and bookshelves, coffered ceilings, and decorative columns are pleasant surprises as you wander the home. Its kitchen is equipped with every creature-comfort imaginable, an island with a surface unit and serving bar, double ovens and a butler's pantry. A built-in message center keeps the family organized. A gallery and a loft – both with overlooks to the main level – are incorporated into the upper floor. ▪

Foundations Available: Basement, Crawl or Slab

*Rear elevation*

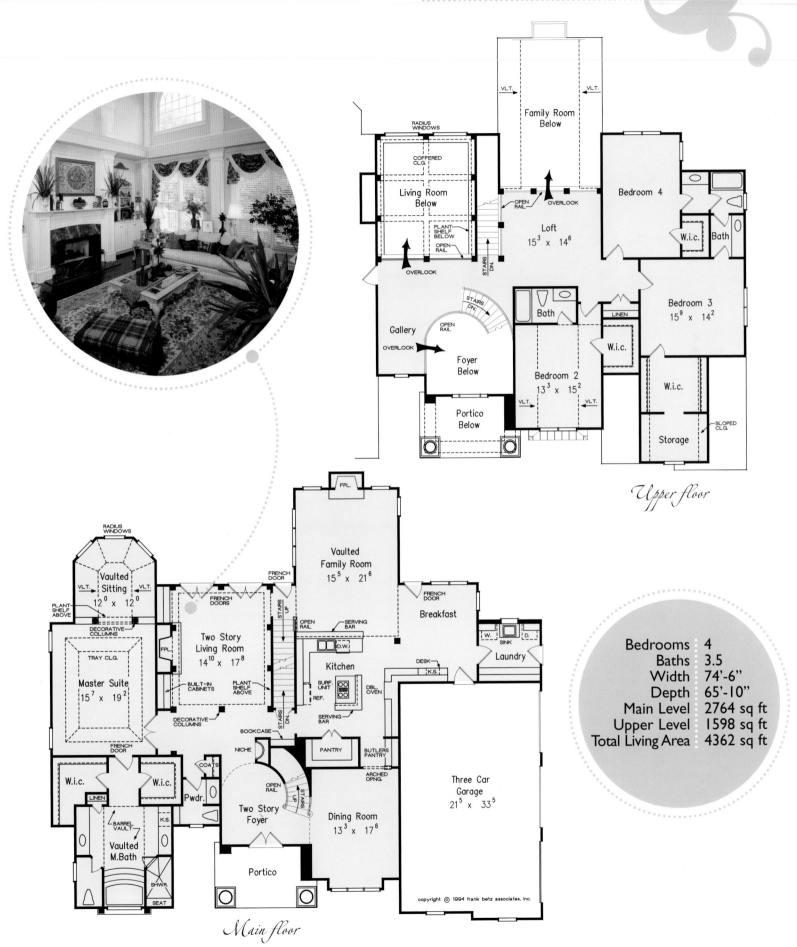

## Upper floor

Family Room Below

RADIUS WINDOWS

COFFERED CLG.

Living Room Below

PLANT SHELF BELOW

OPEN RAIL

OVERLOOK

VLT.    VLT.

OPEN RAIL    OVERLOOK

Loft
15³ x 14⁶

STAIRS DN.

Bedroom 4

W.i.c.    Bath

Gallery

OVERLOOK

OPEN RAIL

STAIRS DN.

Foyer Below

Bath

LINEN

W.i.c.

Bedroom 3
15⁹ x 14²

Bedroom 2
13³ x 15²

W.i.c.

Portico Below

VLT.    VLT.

W.i.c.

Storage

SLOPED CLG.

## Main floor

RADIUS WINDOWS

Vaulted Sitting
12⁰ x 12⁰

VLT.    VLT.

PLANT SHELF ABOVE

DECORATIVE COLUMNS

TRAY CLG.

FPL.

FRENCH DOOR

FRENCH DOORS

Two Story Living Room
14¹⁰ x 17⁸

STAIRS UP

OPEN RAIL

SERVING BAR

D.W.

Vaulted Family Room
15⁵ x 21⁶

FRENCH DOOR

Breakfast

W.    SINK    D.

Laundry

Master Suite
15⁷ x 19²

BUILT-IN CABINETS

PLANT SHELF ABOVE

Kitchen

SURF. UNIT

REF.

DBL. OVEN

DESK

K.S.

FRENCH DOOR

DECORATIVE COLUMNS

STAIRS DN.

BOOKCASE

SERVING BAR

W.i.c.    W.i.c.

LINEN

Pwdr.

BARREL VAULT

K.S.

NICHE

PANTRY

BUTLERS PANTRY

ARCHED OPNG.

Three Car Garage
21⁵ x 33⁵

Vaulted M.Bath

SHWR.

SEAT

COATS

Two Story Foyer

OPEN RAIL

STAIRS UP

Dining Room
13³ x 17⁶

Portico

copyright © 1994 frank betz associates, inc.

| | |
|---|---|
| Bedrooms | 4 |
| Baths | 3.5 |
| Width | 74'-6" |
| Depth | 65'-10" |
| Main Level | 2764 sq ft |
| Upper Level | 1598 sq ft |
| Total Living Area | 4362 sq ft |

# Hermitage

Plan Number: MLFB04-792
Price Code: H

This expansive home is perfect for entertaining or for large families. A spacious, amenity-filled kitchen gives way to a vaulted family room complete with its own covered porch. A convenient butler's pantry enhances the formal dining room, while the breakfast room is perfect for a more casual dining atmosphere. An impressive two-story library sits at the front of the home, and is accented by a cozy fireplace. The master suite is truly spectacular, with decorative columns, a double vanity in the bathroom, and separate shower and garden tub. ■

Foundations Available: Basement

*Rear elevation*

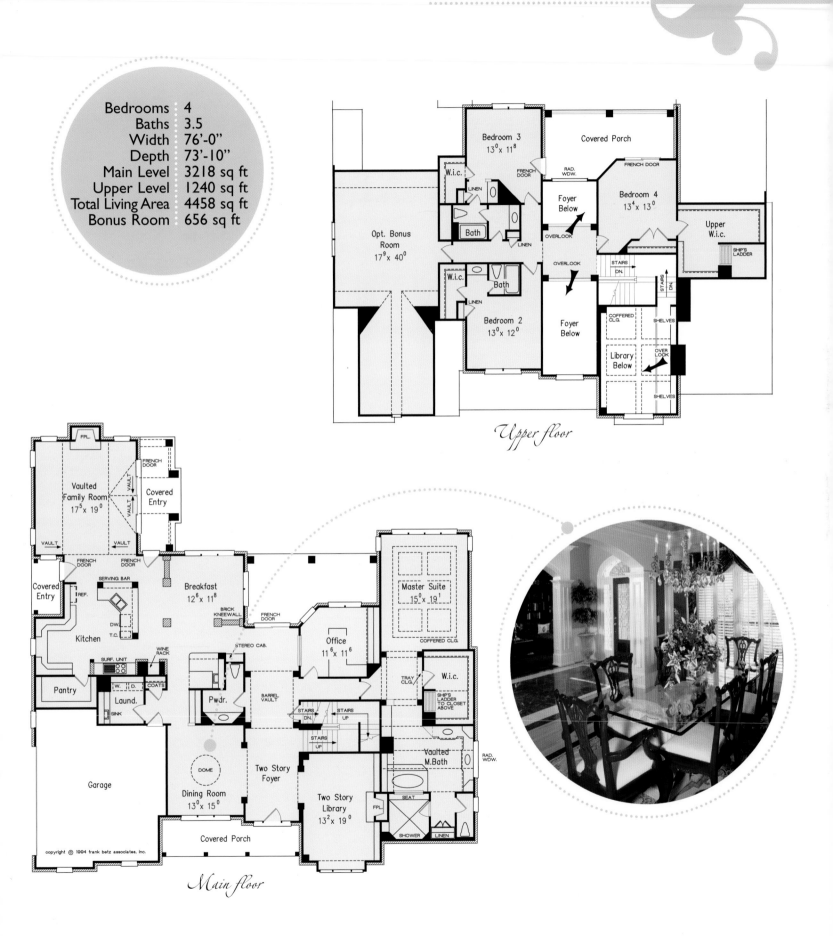

Bedrooms : 4
Baths : 3.5
Width : 76'-0"
Depth : 73'-10"
Main Level : 3218 sq ft
Upper Level : 1240 sq ft
Total Living Area : 4458 sq ft
Bonus Room : 656 sq ft

*Upper floor*

*Main floor*

copyright © 1994 frank betz associates, inc.

# Plan Index

A fireplace with a formal wood mantel and a marble hearth is the focal point in the family room of the Mallory plan. Sunlight fills the room through windows that flank the fireplace.

**See more of the Mallory on page 86.**

# Construction drawing
## Information

### CONSTRUCTION DRAWINGS

Each set of plans from Frank Betz Associates, Inc., will provide you with the necessary information needed to construct a home. The actual number of pages may vary but each set of plans may contain the following information:

**1 FRONT ELEVATIONS/DETAILS**

All plans include the front elevation at 1/4" or 3/16" scale and the sides and rear elevations at 1/8" scale. The elevations show and note the exterior finish materials of the house.

**2 ELEVATIONS/ROOF PLAN**

The side and rear elevations are shown at 1/8" scale. The roof plan is a "bird's eye" view showing the roof pitches, overhangs, ridges, valleys and any saddles. The roof plan may be shown separately or in conjunction with the roof framing plan.

**3 FOUNDATION PLAN**

Every plan is available with a walk-out style basement (three masonry walls and one wood framed rear wall with windows and doors). The basement plans are a 1/4" scale layout of unfinished spaces showing only the necessary 2 x 6 wood framed load-bearing walls. Crawl foundations and/or slab-on-grade foundations are available for many plans. All foundation types are not available for all plans.

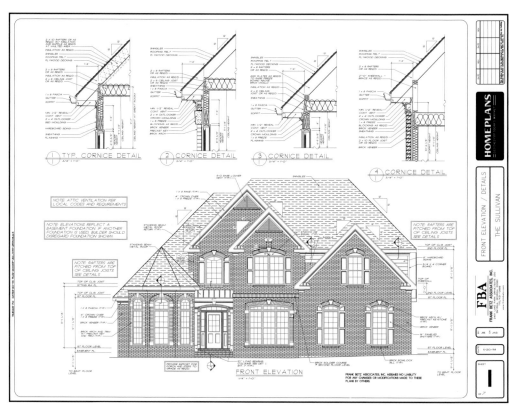

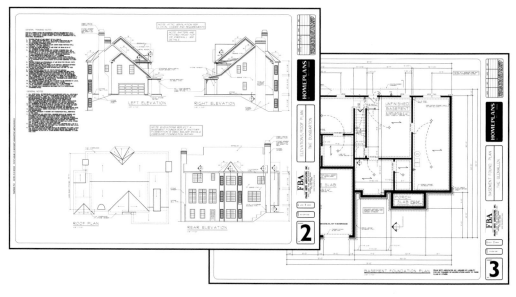

**4  FLOOR PLANS**

Each plan consists of 1/4" or 3/16" scale floor layouts showing the location of walls, doors, windows, plumbing fixtures, cabinetry, stairs and decorative ceilings. The floor plans are complete with dimensions, notes, door/window sizes and schematic electrical layout.

**5  SECTION(S)**

The building sections are drawings which take vertical cuts through the house and stairs showing floor, ceiling and roof height information.

**6  KITCHEN AND BATH ELEVATIONS/DETAILS**

The kitchen and bath elevations show the arrangement and size of each cabinet and other fixtures in the room. These drawings give basic information that can be used to create customized layouts with a cabinet manufacturer. Details are included for many interior and exterior conditions to provide more specific construction information.

**7  FIRST AND SECOND FLOOR FRAMING PLANS\***

The floor framing plans show each floor joist indicating the size, spacing and length. All beams are labeled and sized. All of the joists are counted and coordinated with the material list. Each framing plan sheet includes any framing details that are needed (tray details, connection details, etc.). The framing plans are designed using conventional 2 x 10 floor joists or wood I-Joists depending on the span conditions of each home plan.

**8  CEILING JOIST FRAMING\***

The ceiling joist framing plan shows each ceiling joist indicating the size, spacing and length. All beams are labeled and sized. All of the joists are counted and coordinated with the material list.

**9  ROOF FRAMING PLAN\***

The roof framing plan shows each rafter, valley, hip and ridge indicating the size, spacing and length. All beams are labeled and sized. All of the joists are counted and coordinated with the material list.

*\* All Southern Living® plans include the framing information on the main floor plans. Southern Living® plans do not have separate framing sheets.*

**TYPICAL DETAIL SHEETS**

Each plan order includes one set of typical detail sheets that show foundation details, typical wall sections and other framing details. Also included on the detail sheets are miscellaneous interior trim and fireplace details that can be used to customize the home.

# Ordering
## Information

## LICENSING INFORMATION

Each plan purchase includes a non-exclusive, non-transferable license that states the terms of use for our plans. An eight-set package includes a license to build one home and does not allow any changes to be made to the plan(s). The reproducible and CAD packages include licenses that allow the purchaser to build the plan(s) multiple times and allows the purchaser to make changes to the plan.

## SHIPPING INFORMATION

Typically, we ship our orders the following business day after receipt of order. All plans are shipped via Federal Express 2-day or Overnight. Plans must be shipped to a street address as Federal Express will not deliver to a Post Office Box.

## CODE COMPLIANCE

Our plans are drawn to meet the 2000 International Residential Code for One and Two Family Dwellings and the 2000 International Building Code with the Georgia Amendments. Many states and counties amend the code for their area. Each building department's requirements for a permit may vary. Consult your local building officials to determine the plan, code and site requirements. Frank Betz Associates home plans are not stamped by an architect or engineer. Our plans include the drawings typically needed for construction, except site-specific information and heating and cooling requirements. This information, if required, must be provided based on the geographic conditions in your area.

## OUR EXCHANGE POLICY

Plans may be returned for a full refund, less applicable restocking fees and shipping charges, by returning the **unopened** package to our office. No returns will be accepted on open boxes, electronic CAD files, or electronic or printed artwork. Plans may be exchanged within 30 days of purchase. Exchanges are subject to price difference and restocking fees.

## HOW TO ORDER

When placing an order, you may do so online, by mail, fax or phone. To order online visit www.mainfloormastersuites.com and follow the directions to the order form. To speak to a customer-service representative, call 888-717-3003. Orders may be faxed to 770-435-7608 or mailed to Betz Publishing, 2401 Lake Park Drive, Suite 250, Smyrna, Georgia 30080. We accept Visa, Mastercard, American Express and Discover. Orders can also be sent COD for an additional charge. COD orders require certified funds.

## IGNORING COPYRIGHT LAWS CAN BE AN EXPENSIVE MISTAKE

United States copyright laws allow for statutory damages of up to $150,000.00 per incident for copyright infringement involving any of the copyrighted plans found in this publication. The law can be confusing. So, for your own protection, take the time to understand what you can and cannot not do when it comes to house plans. Please call us for more information on copyright laws.